KT-379-862

1000 THINGS YOU SHOULD KNOW ABOUT

BUILDINGS & TRANSPORT

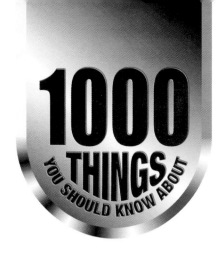

1000 THINGS YOU SHOULD KNOW ABOUT

BUILDINGS & TRANSPORT

John Farndon

Miles Kelly

PUBLISHING

First published in 2000 by
Miles Kelly Publishing Ltd
Bardfield Centre, Great Bardfield, Essex, CM7 4SL

Copyright © Miles Kelly Publishing 2000

6 8 10 9 7

Editorial Director: Anne Marshall
Project Manager: Ian Paulyn
Production: Estela Godoy
Picture Research: Liberty Newton
Written and designed: Barnsbury Books

All rights reserved. No part of this publication may be reproduced,
stored in a retrieval system, or transmitted by any means, electronic,
mechanical, photocopying, recording or otherwise, without the prior
permission of the copyright holder.

British Library Cataloguing-in-Publication Data
A catalogue record for this book is available from the British library

ISBN 1-902947-27-4

Printed in China

CONTENTS

KEY

 Cars

 Trains

 Planes

 Buildings

 Great monuments

 Boats

Cathedrals

- **Cathedrals** are the churches of Christian bishops.
- **The word cathedral** comes from the Greek word for 'seat', *kathedra*.
- **Cathedrals** are typically built in the shape of a cross. The entrance of the cathedral is at the west end.
- **The long end** of the cross is the nave.

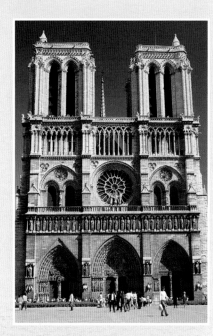

▲ *Paris's famous Notre Dame dates from 1163, but was remodelled in the 1840s by Viollet-le-Duc.*

- The short end, containing the altar and choir stalls, is called the apse. The arms of the cross are called transepts.
- **Canterbury and a few other cathedrals** were built as early as the 6th-century AD. Most European cathedrals were built between 1000 and 1500.
- **Medieval cathedrals** were often built in the 'gothic' style with soaring, pointed arches, tall spires and huge pointed arch windows.
- **Many gothic cathedrals** have beautiful stained-glass windows. Chartres Cathedral in France has 176.
- **The modern Crystal Cathedral** in California is star-shaped and made of glass for TV broadcasts.
- **The world's tallest** cathedral spire is in Ulm, Germany, which is 160.9 m tall.
- **The world's smallest** cathedral is Christ Church in Highlandville, Missouri, USA which is just 4.2 by 5.2 m and holds only 18 people.

The first railways

- **Railways** were invented long before steam power.
- **The Diolkos** was a 6 km long railway that transported boats across the Corinth isthmus in Greece in the 6th-century BC. Trucks pushed by slaves ran in grooves in a limestone track.
- **The Diolkos** ran for over 1300 years until AD 900.
- **Railways** were revived in Europe in the 14th century with wooden trackrails to guide horse and hand carts taking ore out of mines.
- **In the 1700s,** English ironmakers began to make rails of iron. First the rail was wood covered in iron. Then the whole rail was made of iron. Iron wheels with 'flanges' (lips) ran inside the track.

▶ *The Stephensons' 'Rocket' was the most famous early locomotive, winning the first locomotive speed trials at Rainhill in England in 1829.*

- **In 1804** Cornish engineer Richard Trevithick built the first successful steam railway locomotive.
- **Trevithick's** engine pulled a train of five wagons with 9 tonnes of iron and 70 men along 15 km of track at the Pendarren ironworks in Wales.
- **On 27 September 1825** George and Robert Stephenson opened the world's first steam passenger railway, the Stockton and Darlington in England.
- **The gauge (trackwidth)** used for the Stockton and Darlington was 1.44 m, the same length as axles on horse-wagons. This became the standard gauge in the USA and much of Europe.
- **The English-built 'Stourbridge Lion'** was the first full-size steam locomotive to run in the USA. It ran on wooden track in Pennsylvania in 1829.

Controlling a plane

- **A plane** is controlled in the air by moving hinged flaps on its wings and tail.

- **Changing pitch** is when the plane goes nose-up or nose-down to dive or climb.

- **Rolling** is when the plane rolls to one side, dipping one wing or the other.

- **Yawing** is when the plane steers to the left or right like a car.

- **Pitch** is controlled by raising or lowering hinged flaps on the rear wings called elevators.

- **To pitch up** in a small or simple plane, the pilot pulls back on the control column to raise the elevators.

- **Rolling** is controlled by large hinged flaps on the wings called ailerons.

◀ In old-fashioned planes, the pilot controlled the flaps manually by moving a control stick linked to the flaps by cables. In modern planes, the flaps are controlled automatically via electric wires (fly-by-wire) or laser beams (fly-by-light). The flight deck of this plane from 30 years ago has lots of dials to help the pilot. Modern planes have 'glass cockpits', which means they have computer screens.

- **To roll left,** the pilot pushes the control column to the left, which raises the aileron on the left wing and lowers it on the right.

- **Yawing** is controlled by the vertical hinged flap on the tail called the rudder.

- **To yaw left,** the pilot pushes the foot-operated rudder bar forward with his left foot, to swing the rudder left.

Trucks

- **Trucks or lorries** can weigh 40 tonnes or more – maybe as much as 50 cars.

- **Cars** are powered by petrol engines; trucks are typically powered by diesel engines.

- **Cars** typically have five forward gears; trucks often have as many as 16.

- **Cars** typically have four wheels. Trucks often have 12 or 16 to help spread the load.

- **Many trucks** have the same basic cab and chassis (the framework supporting the body). Different bodies are fitted on to the chassis to suit the load.

- **Some trucks** are in two parts, hinged at the join. These are called articulated trucks.

- **The cab and engine** of an articulated truck is called the tractor unit. The load is carried in the trailer.

- **In Australia** one tractor may pull several trailers in a 'road-train' along the long, straight desert roads.

▲ This 14-wheel tanker is articulated, and the tank and tractor unit can be separated.

- **The longest truck** is the Arctic Snow Train, first made for the US army. This is 174 m long and has 54 wheels.

- **Large trucks** are sometimes called 'juggernauts'. Juggernaut was a form of the Hindu god Vishnu who rode a huge chariot, supposed by Europeans to crush people beneath its wheels.

Mosques

- **The word 'mosque'** comes from the Arabic *masjid*, which means a place of kneeling.

- **Mosques** are places where Muslims worship. Muslims can worship anywhere clean. So a mosque can be just a stick in the sand to mark out a space for praying or even just a mat. But many mosques are beautiful buildings.

- **Cathedral or Friday** mosques are large

▲ *Typically minarets on mosques have onion-shaped roofs.*

mosques big enough to hold all the adult Muslims in the area.

- **Typically** mosques have a courtyard surrounded by four walls called iwans. There is often a fountain or fuawara at the centre for ceremonial washing.

- **The mihrab** is a decorative niche on the inner wall closest to the city of Mecca that muslims face when praying.

- **The mimbar** is the stone or wooden pulpit where the Imam leads the people in prayer.

- **Most mosques** have two to six tall pointed towers which are called minarets.

- **On each minaret** is a balcony from which muezzin (criers) call the faithful to prayer five times a day.

- **Minarets** may have been inspired by the Pharos, the famous lighthouse at Alexandria in Egypt.

- **There are** no paintings or statues in mosques, only abstract patterns, often made of tiles.

Motorbikes

▲ *Many enthusiasts still ride motorbikes like this from the 1930s when motorcycling was in its heyday.*

- **The first petrol engine** motorbike was built by Gottlieb Daimler in Germany in 1885.

- **Most small motorbikes** have a two-stroke petrol engine, typically air-cooled and quite noisy.

- **Most larger motorbikes** have four-stroke petrol engines, typically water-cooled.

- **On most bikes** the engine drives the rear wheel via a chain; on some the drive is via a shaft.

- **A trail bike** is a bike with a high mounted frame and chunky tyres, designed to be ridden over rough tracks.

- **Motorbikes** with engines smaller than 50cc may be called mopeds, because in the past they had pedals as well as an engine.

- **The biggest motorbikes** have engines of around 1200cc.

- **The most famous** motorbike race in the world is the Isle of Man TT, or Tourist Trophy.

- **In Speedway,** bikes with no brakes or gears are raced round dirt tracks.

★ **STAR FACT** ★
The first motorbike was steam powered, and built by the Michaux brothers in 1868.

Building of the railways

- **On the 15th September 1830** the world's first major passenger railway opened between Liverpool and Manchester.

- **At the opening** of the Liverpool and Manchester railway, government minister William Huskisson was the first railway casualty, killed by the locomotive.

- **In 1831** the Best Friend started a regular train service between Charleston and Hamburg, South Carolina in the USA.

- **By 1835** there were over 1600 km of railway in the USA.

- **In Britain** railway building became a mania in the 1840s.

- **Hundreds of acts** of parliament gave railway companies the powers to carve their way through cities

◀ *The new railways often meant demolishing huge strips through cities to lay track into stations.*

and the countryside .

- **By the late 1840s** Great Western Railway trains were able to average well over 100 km/h all the way from London to Exeter via Bristol, completing the 300 odd km journey in under 4 hours.

- **On 10th May 1869** railways from either side of the United States met at Promontory, Utah, giving North America the first transcontinental railway.

- **The British** built 40,000 km of railways in India in the 1880s and 90s.

- **Vast armies of men** worked on building the railways – 45,000 on the London and Southampton railway alone.

Early boats

- **The Aborigines** arrived by boat in Australia at least 50,000 years ago, as cave paintings show.

- **The oldest remains** of boats are 8000 or so years old, like the 4 m canoe found at Pesse in the Netherlands.

- **Many early canoes** were simply hollowed out logs, called dugouts.

- **The islands of the Pacific** were probably colonized by dugouts, stabilized by attaching an outrigger (an extra float on the side) or adding extra hulls.

- **Lighter canoes** could be made by stretching animal skins over a light frame of bent wood.

- **4000 years ago,** Ancient Egyptians were making ships over 30 m long by interlocking planks of wood and lashing them together with tough grass rope.

- **By 1000 BC,** Phoenician traders were sailing into the Atlantic in ships made of planks of Cedar trees.

▲◀ *Outriggers (above) were used to colonize the Pacific tens of thousands of years ago. But many early boats like the Welsh coracle (left) were made by stretching animal skins over a wooden frame.*

- **All early boats** were driven by hand – using either a pole pushed along the bottom, or a paddle.

- **Sails** were first used 7000 years ago in Mesopotamia on reed trading boats.

- **The first known picture** of a sail is 5500 years old and comes from Egypt.

Castles

- **Castles** were the fortress homes of powerful men such as kings and dukes in the Middle Ages. The castle acted as a stronghold for commanding the country around it. They were also barracks for troops, prisons, armouries and centres of local government.

- **The first castles,** in the 11th century, had a high earth mound called a motte, topped by a wooden tower. Around this was an enclosure called a bailey, protected by a fence of wooden stakes and a ditch.

- **From the 12th century** the tower was built of stone and called a keep or donjon. This was the last refuge in an attack. Soon the wooden fences were replaced by thick stone walls and strong towers.

- **Walls and towers** were topped by battlements – low walls with gaps for defenders to fire weapons from.

- **Castles evolved** from a simple square tower to elaborate rings of fortifications. The entrance or gatehouse was equipped with booby traps.

- **From the 13th century** the ditch around the castle was often dug deep, filled with water and called a moat. This stopped enemies from sapping (digging under the walls).

- **Many castles** in England and Wales were first built by the Norman conquerors in the 11th century, including Windsor Castle which dates from 1070.

- **In early castles** there was just a single great hall. Later castles had extra small rooms for the lord and lady, such as the solar, which had windows.

- **The gong farmer** was the man who had to clean out the pit at the bottom of the garderobe (toilet shute).

- **An attack on a castle** was called a siege and could last many months, or even years.

▼ This shows some of the main features of a medieval castle. Very few castles had all of these features. Innovations were constantly being added over the centuries as attackers came up with better ways of breaching the defences and defenders found ways to hold them at bay.

The largest room was the great hall where people ate, slept and carried out castle business

A few castles had private rooms on the third floor for the lord and his lady. Here the lady had her room or bower

Staircases spiralled clockwise so that a defender could retreat, swinging his sword in his right hand

Chapel

Undercroft

Keep

Inner bailey

Outer bailey

Drawbridge – a wooden bridge that was hauled up when the castle was attacked

Drop-gate or portcullis

Archers fire through a slit or loop

Moat

Gatehouse

Galleons

◄ *In this replica of a ship from around 1600, the tall stern castle where the captain lived is clearly visible.*

● **Galleons** were huge sailing ships that were built from the mid 1500s onwards.

● **Galleons** had tall structures called castles at either end.

● **The front castle** was called the forecastle or fo'c'sle (said folk-sel).

● **The rear castle** was called the stern castle and it housed elaborate living quarters for the officers.

The crew lived in crowded rows below deck.

● **The stern of the ship** was often ornately carved and painted in gold and bright colours.

● **A galleon** had three tall masts – the foremast, the mainmast and the mizzenmast at the rear.

● **Galleons** were both warships and trading boats and carried vast numbers of cannon and troops.

● **In the 1500s,** enormous Spanish galleons crossed the Atlantic carrying gold from the Americas to Spain.

● **When the Spanish Armada** of galleons was sent to attack England in 1588, they were outfought by the smaller but faster and lighter English ships, despite their heavy armament.

★ **STAR FACT** ★
The biggest Spanish galleons weighed well over 1000 tonnes.

The Colosseum

● **The Colosseum** was a huge stone sports arena built in Ancient Rome.

● **It was 189 m long,** 156 m wide, and 52 m high.

● **It held** up to 73,000 spectators who entered through 80 entrances. Each spectator had a ticket corresponding to one of the 76 arcades.

● **The sports** included fights between gladiators with swords, nets and other weapons who fought to the death, or fought against lions and other wild beasts.

● **Counterweighted** doors allowed 64 wild beasts to be released from their cages simultaneously.

● **It took just eight years** – from around AD 70 to AD 78 – to build the Colosseum.

● **To build it** the Romans brought almost a quarter of a million tonnes of stone by barge from quarries 20 km outside Rome.

● **During construction,** a cart carrying a tonne of stone would have left the riverside wharves every seven

▲ *The Colosseum in Rome was one of the greatest buildings of the ancient world.*

minutes on the 1.5 km journey to the site.

● **A huge awning** called a velarium, supported by 240 masts, protected the arena from bad weather.

● **Its opening was celebrated** by spectacular games lasting 100 days.

Tractors

- **Tractors** are motor vehicles used mostly on farms for pulling or pushing machines such as ploughs.

- **Tractors** are also used in factories, by the army, for logging and for clearing snow.

- **Steam-powered tractors** called 'traction engines' were introduced in 1834 by Walter Hancock.

- **Traction-engines** could pull up to 40 ploughs at once via long chains, but they were too cumbersome to be practical in hilly country.

- **Petrol-powered tractors** were introduced in the 1890s but they were not powerful enough for most farm work.

- **The first all-purpose** farm tractors appeared in the 1920s and soon began to replace horses and oxen.

> ★ STAR FACT ★
> There are now well over 16 million tractors around the world.

▲ *Modern tractors can be adapted to operate all kinds of devices, including this haybailer, via the power take-off.*

- **Ploughs and other equipment** are drawn along via the drawbar on the back of the tractor.

- **The power take-off** or PTO allows the tractor's engine to power equipment such as potato diggers.

- **25% of all tractors** are in the USA.

The Age of Sail

- **East Indiamen** were ships that carried ivory, silks and spices to Europe from India, China and the East Indies.

- **By 1800** Indiamen could carry 1000 tonnes of cargo.

- **Packet ships** were ships that provided a regular service across the Atlantic between Europe and the USA – no matter whether they had a full load or not.

- **The first packet service** began in 1818 with the Black Ball Line from Liverpool to New York. Red Star and Swallowtail followed.

◀ *The tea clippers of the mid-1800s were the pinnacle of sailing ship technology, able to carry thousands of tonnes of tea at speeds of 20 knots or more.*

- **Clippers** were the big, fast sailing ships that 'clipped off' time as they raced to get cargoes of tea from China and India back first to markets in Europe and the USA.

- **Clippers** had slender hulls, tall masts and up to 35 sails.

- **Clippers could reach** speeds of 30 knots (55 km/h). Many could sail from New York, round South America, to San Francisco in under 100 days.

- **In 1866** the clippers *Taeping*, *Serica* and *Ariel* raced 25,700 km from Foochow in China to London in 99 days.

- **Canadian Donald Mckay** of Boston, Massachusetts, was the greatest clipper builder. His ship the *Great Republic* of 1853 was the biggest sailing ship of its time, over 100 m long and able to carry 4000 tonnes of cargo.

- **A famous clipper,** the *Cutty Sark*, built in 1869 is preserved at Greenwich, London. Its name is Scottish for 'short shirt' and comes from the witch in Robert Burns's poem *Tam O'Shanter*.

Parachutes, hang-gliders

- **Leonardo da Vinci** drew a design for a parachute around 1500.

- **The first human parachute drop** was made by Jacques Garnerin from a balloon over Paris in 1797.

- **Folding parachutes** were used first in the USA in 1880.

- **Early parachutes** were made of canvas, then silk. Modern parachutes are made of nylon, stitched in panels to limit tears to a small area.

- **Until recently** parachutes were shaped like umbrellas; now most are 'parafoils' – wing-shaped.

- **Drogues** are parachutes thrown out by jet planes and high-speed cars to slow them down.

- **German Otto Lilienthal** flew his own canvas and wood hang-gliders in the 1890s.

- **Modern hang-gliding** began with the fabric delta

◀ Parachutes really came into their own with the massive parachute drops of troops into battle during World War II.

(triangular) wing design developed by the American Francis Rogallo in the 1940s.

- **Today's hang-gliders** are made by stretching nylon over a very light and strong nylon and kevlar frame. They combine long aeroplane-like wings and a double skin of fabric to achieve very long flights.

- **The first hang-gliders** achieved a glide ratio of 1:2.5 – that is, they travelled only 2.5 m forward for every 1 m that they dropped. Today's hang-gliders give glide ratios of 1:14 or better.

Skyscrapers

- **The first skyscrapers** were built in Chicago and New York in the 1880s.

- **A crucial step** in the development of skyscrapers was the invention of the fast safety lift by US engineer Elisha Otis (1811-61) in 1857.

- **The Home Insurance Building** in Chicago, built in 1885, was one of the first skyscrapers.

- **In buildings** over 40-storeys high, the weight of the building is less important in terms of strength than the wind load (the force of the wind against the building).

- **The Empire State Building,** built in New York in 1931, was for decades the world's tallest building at 381 m.

- **The tallest building** in America is the 442 m-high Sears Tower in Chicago, built in 1974.

> **! NEWS FLASH !**
> The Landmark Tower in Kowloon, Hong Kong, could be 574 m high.

▶ New York's Manhattan has more skyscrapers than anywhere else in the world.

- **The world's tallest building** is the 452 m Petronas twin towers in Kuala Lumpur, Malaysia.

- **If the Grollo Tower** is built in Melbourne Australia it will be 560 m high.

- **An early concept** design has been presented for a Tokyo building measuring 4000 m!

St Sophia

- **Saint or Hagia Sophia** was built as an ancient Christian cathedral in Istanbul in Turkey (Roman 'Byzantium').

- **Hagia Sophia** is Greek for 'holy wisdom'.

- **St Sophia** was built between AD 532 and AD 537, when Istanbul was called Constantinople.

- **The great Byzantine** emperor Justinian I ordered the building of St Sophia after a fire destroyed an earlier church on the site.

- **St Sophia** was designed by the brilliant Byzantine architects Anthemius of Tralles and Isidorus of Miletus.

- **The main structure** is a framework of arches and vaults (high arched ceilings).

- **The dome** is 31 m across and 56 m high. It is supported by four triangular brick pillars called pendentives.

- **St Sophia is decorated** with marble veneers and mosaics of Mary, Christ, angels and bishops.

- **In 1453** the Ottoman Turks took the city and converted St Sophia to a mosque. They plastered over the mosaics and added four minarets on the outside.

- **In 1935** St Sophia was converted into a museum and the mosaics were uncovered.

▼ Istanbul's St Sophia is one of the world's oldest cathedrals and one of the most remarkable pieces of ancient architecture.

Viking longships

- **Viking longships** were the long narrow boats built by the Viking warriors of Scandinavia around AD 1000.

- **A virtually** intact ship was found in 1880 at Gokstad near Oseberg in Norway. A king was buried inside it.

- **Longships** were very fast, light and seaworthy.

▲ The Gokstad ship dates from c. AD 900.

- They carried the Viking explorer Leif Ericsson all the way across the Atlantic to North America.

- **In 1893** a replica of the Gokstad ship sailed across the Atlantic in 28 days.

- **Some Viking longships** were up to 30 m long and 17 m across and could carry 200 warriors.

- **At sea** longships relied on a single square sail made up from strips of woollen cloth; on rivers and in calm they used oar-power, with 20–30 rowers on each side.

- **Their ships' shallow build** allowed the Vikings to make raids far up shallow rivers.

- **The prow curved** up to a carved dragon head.

- **Longships** were for carrying warriors on raids, but the Vikings also built wider, deeper 'knorrs' for trade and small rowing boats called 'faerings'.

- **The Viking** ships were very stable because they had a keel, a wooden board about 17 m long and 45 cm deep, along the bottom of the boat.

Diesel trains

★ STAR FACT ★
In 1987, a British Rail diesel train set a world
diesel speed record of nearly 240 km/h.

- **The diesel engine** was invented by Rudolf Diesel in 1892 and experiments with diesel locomotives started soon after. The first great success was the *Flying Hamburger* which ran from Berlin to Hamburg in the 1930s at speeds of 125 km/h. Diesel took over from steam in the 1950s and 1960s.

- **Diesel locomotives** are really electric locomotives that carry their own power plant. The wheels are driven by an electric motor which is supplied with electricity by the locomotive's diesel engine.

- **The power output of a diesel** engine is limited, so high-speed trains are electric – but diesels can supply their own electricity so need no trackside cables.

- **There are two other kinds** of diesel apart from diesel-electrics: diesel-hydraulic and diesel-mechanical.

- **In diesel-hydraulics,** the power from the diesel engine is connected to the wheels via a torque converter, which is a turbine driven round by fluid.

- **In diesel-mechanicals,** the power is transmitted from the diesel engine to the wheels via gears and shafts. This only works for small locomotives.

- **Diesel locomotives** may be made up from one or more separate units. An A unit holds the driver's cab and leads the train. A B unit simply holds an engine.

- **A typical diesel** for fast, heavy trains or for trains going over mountains may consist of one A unit and six B units.

- **The usual maximum** power output from a single diesel locomotive is about 3500–4000 horsepower. In Russia, several 3000-horsepower units are joined together to make 12,000-horsepower locomotives.

▼ This is a typical British diesel-electric locomotive from the 1960s. It has a cab at both ends so that it can be operated in either direction. This is one of the older generation of diesel-electrics that use DC (Direct Current) generators. DC generators give a current that flows in only one direction. Most newer engines take advantage of electronic devices called rectifiers to use the current from an AC (Alternating Current) generator. An AC generator gives a current that swaps direction many times a second. The rectifiers convert this into a direct current. AC generators are far more powerful and efficient.

Diesel engine in which diesel fuel is squeezed inside cylinders until it bursts into flame. The expansion of the fuel as it burns provides the engine's power

Fuel tank carrying diesel fuel. Because a diesel train carries its fuel on board, it is entirely independent, unlike electric locomotives

Cooling fan

Locomotive driving wheels, turned by the power of the electricity generator

Driver's cab

Direct Current electricity generator turned by the power of the diesel engine

Supersonic planes

▶ *The Anglo-French Concorde, created in 1969, was the most popular supersonic airliner for many years.*

! NEWS FLASH !
The Soviet Tupolev Tu-144 of 1968 was the very first supersonic jetliner.

- **Supersonic planes** travel faster than the speed of sound.

- **The speed of sound** is about 1220 km/h at sea level at 15°C.

- **Sound travels** slower higher up, so the speed of sound is about 1060 km/h at 12,000 m.

- **Supersonic** plane speeds are given in Mach numbers. These are the speed of the plane divided by the speed of sound at the plane's altitude.

- **A plane flying** at 1500 km/h at 12,000 m, where the speed of sound is 1060 km/h, is at Mach 1.46.

- **A plane flying** at supersonic speeds builds up shock waves in front and behind because it keeps catching up and compressing the sound waves in front of it.

- **The double shock waves** create a sharp crack called a sonic boom that is heard on the ground. Two booms can often be heard a second or two apart.

- **In 1947** Chuck Yeager of the USAF made the first supersonic flight in the Bell X-1 rocket plane. The X-15 rocket plane later reached speeds faster than Mach 6. Speeds faster than Mach 5 are called hypersonic.

- **The first jet plane** to fly supersonic was the F-100 Super Sabre fighter of 1953. The first supersonic bomber was the USAF's Convair B-58 Hustler of 1956.

Famous castles

▲ *Eilean Donan in Scotland was used in the film 'Braveheart'.*

- **The Arab Gormaz Castle** in the Castile region of Spain is Western Europe's biggest and oldest castle. It was started in AD 956 by Caliph Al-Hakam II. It is 1 km round and over 400 m across.

- **Bran Castle** in Romania was built in 1212 by Teutonic (German) knights. In the 1450s, it was one of the castles of Vlad the Impaler, the original Count Dracula.

- **Windsor Castle** in England has been one of the main homes of English kings and queens since the 1100s.

- **Malbork Castle** near Gdansk in Poland is the biggest medieval castle, built by the Teutonic knights in 1309.

- **Germany's Neuschwanstein** castle was started in 1869 by 'Mad' King Ludwig II. Its name means 'new swan castle' after Swan Knight in Wagner's opera *Lohengrin*.

- **Neuschwanstein** is the model for the castle in Walt Disney's cartoon film *Sleeping Beauty*.

- **15th century Blarney Castle** in Ireland is home to the famous 'Blarney stone'. Kissing the stone is said to give people the 'gift of the gab' (fast and fluent talk).

- **Tintagel Castle** in Cornwall is where legend says the mythical King Arthur was conceived.

- **Colditz Castle** in Germany was a notorious prison camp in World War II.

- **Carcassone** in southern France is a whole town fortified by Catholics c.1220 against those of the Cathar religion.

Golden Gate Bridge

- **The Golden Gate Bridge** spans the entrance to San Francisco Bay in California, USA.

- **The Golden Gate Bridge** is one of the world's largest suspension bridges.

◀ *San Francisco's Golden Gate Bridge is one of the most beautiful – and busiest – bridges in the world.*

! NEWS FLASH !
The tower's foundations are being reinforced to withstand earthquakes.

- **The total length** of the bridge is 2737 m.

- **The towers** at either end are 340 m high. The suspended span between the towers is 1280 m, one of the longest in the world.

- **The roadway is** 67 m above the water, although this varies according to the tide.

- **The Golden Gate Bridge** was designed by Joseph Baerman Strauss and built for $35 million, a third of the original cost estimate.

- **The bridge** was opened to traffic on 27 May 1937.

- **The bridge** carries two six-lane highways and pedestrian paths.

- **The bridge** is double-deck, carrying traffic one way on the upper deck and the other way on the lower deck.

Junks

- **Junks** are wooden sailing boats that have been used in China and the Far East for thousands of years.

- **Typical junks** have a broad flat bow (front).

- **Typical junks** have a broad, high stern castle (rear).

- **Junks have lugsails.** These are triangular sails arranged almost in line with the boat, allowing the boat to sail almost into the wind – unlike the square sails of early European boats which only worked with the wind behind.

- **The Chinese** are believed to have invented lugsails.

- **By the 1400s,** the Chinese were building junks 150 m long and almost 100 m wide – much bigger than any sailing ship yet built in Europe.

- **In 1405** the Chinese admiral Cheng Ho led a fleet of exploration through the Indian Ocean. His fleet consisted of 62 large junks and 255 small junks. Each of the large junks was gigantic compared with Columbus's *Santa Maria*. The biggest junk was over

1500 tonnes – the *Santa Maria* was only 98 tonnes.

- **Between 1790 and 1810,** traders in the South Seas were terrorized by vast fleets of pirate junks, led by the female pirate Cheng I Sao.

- **Nowadays** most junks are motorized.

- **Junks** are often moored permanently as homes.

▶ *Most sailing junks have two or three masts. Some have more. The sails are made from cotton and supported by bamboo struts.*

Fighters of World War II

Radio aerial

All metal wings with a wingspan of 10 m

Bulletproof windshield

Self-sealing fuel tanks

Four machine guns in each wing

One 20 mm cannon in each wing

1030 hp Rolls-Royce Merlin engine capable of powering the plane to over 520 km/h

Three-blade propeller

◀ Along with the Spitfire, the Hurricane was the mainstay of the British defence against the German air invasion in the Battle of Britain in 1940. Hurricanes and Spitfires would have spectacular aerial 'dogfights' with the Me 109s and FW 190s escorting the German bombers. The sturdy Hurricane proved a highly effective fighter plane.

> ★ STAR FACT ★
> The 'Night Witches' were a crack Soviet squadron of female fighter pilots who flew night raids on the Germans in the Caucasus Mountains.

▲ In the dogfights of the Battle of Britain, the Spitfire's 650 km/h top speed and amazing agility proved decisive.

- **World War II** fighter planes were sleek monoplanes (single-winged aircraft) very different from the biplanes of World War I. Many were developed from racing machines of the 1920s and 1930s.

- **The most famous** British plane was the Supermarine Spitfire. This was developed from the S.6B seaplane which won the coveted Schneider trophy in the late 1920s.

- **The most famous American** fighter was the North American P-51 Mustang, which could reach speeds of over 700 km/h and had a range of 1700 km. It was widely used as an escort for bombers.

- **In the Pacific** US planes like the Grumman Wildcat and Hellcat fought against the fast and highly manoeuvrable Japanese Mitsubishi A6M 'Zero'.

- **The most famous German** fighter was the fast, agile Messerschmitt Bf 109. This was the plane flown by German ace Erich Hartmann, who shot down 352 enemy planes. Over 33,000 Me 109s were made during the war.

- **Me 109s** were nicknamed by model. The Bf109E was the Emil. The Bf109G was the Gustav.

- **The German Focke-Wulf 190** had a big BMW radial engine that enabled it to climb over 1100 km a minute.

- **The most famous Soviet** fighter was the MiG LaGG-3 Interceptor, flown by Soviet air ace Ivan Kozhedub who shot down 62 German planes.

- **The British Hawker Hurricane** was more old-fashioned, slower and less famous than the Spitfire, but its reliability made it highly effective. Hurricanes actually destroyed more enemy aircraft than Spitfires.

The Benz

- **Karl Benz (1844-1929)** and his wife Berta were the German creators of the first successful petrol-driven car in 1885.

- **At the age of 16,** before the first petrol-powered cart was built, Karl Benz dreamed of 'a unit that could supplant the steam engine'.

- **Karl and Berta Benz** began developing their car in the 1870s, while trying to earn money from a tin-making business. By 1880, they were so penniless they could barely afford to eat everyday.

- **Their first car** was a small tricycle, but had a water-cooled four-stroke engine with electric ignition.

▶ *The Benz tricycle was the world's first successful petrol-driven car.*

- **Karl Benz** tested the car round the streets of their home town of Mannheim after dark to avoid scaring people.

- **Berta Benz** recharged the car's battery after each trip by pedalling a dynamo attached to her sewing machine.

- **Berta Benz** secretly made the first long, 100 km journey in the car, without Karl knowing. On the journey to her home in Pforzheim, she had to clear the fuel-line with a hairpin and use her garters to cure an electrical short.

- **The Benz** caused a stir when shown at the Paris World Fair in 1889.

- **Backed by F. von Fischer** and Julian Ganss, Benz began making his cars for sale in 1889 – the first cars ever made for sale.

- **By 1900** Benz was making over 600 cars a year.

Stonehenge

- **Stonehenge** is an ancient stone monument in southern England made from circles of huge rough-cut stones.

- **The main circle of stones** or 'sarsens' is a ring of 30 huge upright stones, joined at the top by 30 lintels. Many of these sarsens have now fallen or been looted.

- **Inside the sarsen ring** are five 'doorways' called trilithons, each made with three gigantic stones, weighing up to 40 tonnes each.

- **In between** are rings of smaller bluestones.

- **The bluestones** come from the Preseli Hills in Wales, 240 km away. Archaeologists puzzle over how they were carried here.

▶ *Experiments have shown a team of 150 people could haul the stones upright, but dragging them to the site on greased wooden sleds must have been a huge undertaking.*

- **At the centre** is a single tall stone, called the Heel Stone.

- **Stonehenge was built** in three phases between 2950 BC and 1600 BC, starting with just a huge earth ring.

- **Archaeologists** believe it was a gathering place and a site for religious ceremonies for Bronze Age people.

- **Newman, Thom and Hawkins** have shown the layout of the stones ties in with astronomical events.

- **At sunrise on midsummer's day** (the solstice), the sun shines directly along the avenue to the Heel Stone.

Warplanes

◀ Pilots flying modern jets fly at supersonic speeds aided by laser-guided weapons, night-vision goggles and other high-tech equipment.

- **The 870 km/h** German Messerschmitt Me 262 was the first jet fighter. It had straight wings like propeller planes.

- **The Lockheed Shooting Star** was the first successful US jet fighter.

- **The Korean War** of the 1950s saw the first major combat between jet fighters. Most now had swept-back wings, like the Russian MiG-15 and the US F-86 Sabre.

- **In 1954** Boeing introduced the B-52 Superfortress, still the USAF's main bomber because of its huge bomb-carrying capacity.

- **In the 1950s** aircraft began flying close to the ground to avoid detection by radar. On modern planes like the Lockheed F-111 a computer radar system flies the plane automatically at a steady height over hills and valleys.

- **The Hawker Harrier** of 1968 was the only successful 'jump jet' with swivelling jets for vertical take-off (VTOL).

- **Airborne Early Warning** systems (AEWs) detect low-flying aircraft. To evade them, the Americans began developing 'stealth' systems like RCS and RAM.

- **RCS** or Radar Cross Section means altering the plane's shape to make it less obvious to radar. RAM (Radar Absorbent Material) is a coating that doesn't reflect radar.

- **In 1988** the US unveiled its first 'stealth' bomber, the B-2, codenamed Have Blue. The F117 stealth fighter followed.

- **The 2500 km/h Russian Sukhoi S-37** Berkut ('golden eagle') of 1997 uses Forward Swept Wings (FSW) for maximum agility, rather than stealth technology.

Gears

▲ Gears are used in a huge range of machines, from watches to motorbikes, for transmitting movement from one shaft to another.

- **Gears** are pairs of toothed wheels that interlock and so transmit power from one shaft to another.

- **The first gears** were wooden, with wooden teeth. By the 6th century AD, wooden gears of all kinds were used in windmills, watermills and winches.

- **Metal gears** appeared in 87 BC and were later used for clocks. Today, all gears are metal and made on a 'gear-hobbing' machine.

- **Simple gears** are wheels with straight cut teeth.

- **Helical gears** have slanting rather than straight teeth, and run smoother. The gears in cars are helical.

- **Bevel or mitre gears** are cone-shaped, allowing shafts to interlock at right angles.

- **In worm gears** one big helical gear interlocks with a long spiral gear on a shaft at right angles.

- **Planetary gears** have a number of gear wheels called spurs or planets that rotate around a central 'sun' gear.

- **In a planetary gear** the planet and sun gear all rotate within a ring called an annulus.

> ★ STAR FACT ★
> Automatic gearboxes in cars use planetary or epicyclic gears.

Arches

- **Before arches,** door openings were just two uprights spanned by a straight piece of wood or stone called a lintel.

- **Arches** replace a straight lintel with a curve. Curved arches can take more weight than a lintel, because downwards weight makes a lintel snap in the middle.

- **The Romans** were the first to use round arches, so round arches are called Roman or Romanesque arches.

- **Roman arches** were built from blocks of stone called voussoirs. They were built up from each side on a semi-circular wooden frame (later removed). A central wedge or keystone is slotted in at the top to hold them together.

- **The posts** supporting arches are called piers. The top of each post is called a springer.

◄ *The famous Arc de Triomphe in Paris was commissioned by Napoleon in 1806 in the style of the triumphal arches built in Ancient Rome to celebrate great victories.*

- **Pointed arches** were first used in Arab mosques like the Dome of the Rock in the 7th century.

- **Pointed arches** were brought to Europe from the Middle East by Crusader knights in the 1100s and put in churches to become part of the gothic style.

- **Horseshoe arches** are used in islamic buildings all round the world.

- **The sides** of an ogee arch are S-shaped. Tudor arches are flattened ogees.

- **The world's biggest free-standing arch** is the Gateway to the West arch in St Louis, Missouri, USA. Completed in 1965, this arch is 192 m high and 192 m across.

Record breaking trains

- **The fastest steam train** ever was by Gresley-designed steam engine *Mallard* pulling seven coaches on 3 July 1938, (see steam locomotives). It travelled at 201 km/h.

- **The most powerful** steam loco was the US Virginian Railway's No.700. It pulled with a force of over 90,000 kg.

- **The heaviest trains** ever pulled by a single locomotive were 250-truck trains that ran on the Erie Railroad in the USA from 1914 to 1929. They weighed over 15,000 tonnes.

- **The longest train** was a 7.3 km 660-truck train that ran from Saldanha to Sishen in South Africa on 26 Aug 1989.

- **The longest passenger train** was a 1732 m 70-coach train from Ghent to Ostend in Belgium on 27 April 1991.

- **The fastest diesel train** was 248 km/h by a British Rail Intercity 125 between Darlington and York on 1 November 1987.

- **The fastest scheduled service** is the Hiroshima-Kokura

bullet train in Japan which covers 192 km in 44 minutes at an average 261.8 km/h.

- **The TGV** from Lille to Roissy in France covers 203 km in 48 mins at an average 254.3 km/h.

- **The fastest train speed ever** was 515.3 km/h by the TGV between Courtalain and Tours, France 18 May 1990.

- **The fastest speed on rail** was 9851 km/h by a rocket sled on White Sands Missile Range, New Mexico in Oct 1982.

▼ *TGV Atlantiques often hit 300 km/h on the French part of the Eurostar run from Paris to London.*

Supercars

▲ *The Porsche 911 is one of the classic supercars, first introduced in 1964, but still looking sleek many years later.*

- **The Mercedes Benz 300SL** of 1952 was one of the first supercars of the post-war years, famous for its stylish flip-up 'Gullwing' doors.

- **The Jaguar E-type** was the star car of the early 1960s with incredibly sleek lines and 250 km/h performance.

- **The Ford Mustang** was one of the first young and lively 'pony' cars, introduced in 1964.

- **The Aston Martin DB6** was the classic supercar of the late 1960s, driven by film spy James Bond.

- **The Porsche 911 turbo** was the fastest accelerating production car for almost 20 years after its launch in 1975, scorching from 0 to 100 km/h in 5.4 seconds.

- **The Lamborghini** Countach was the fastest supercar of the 1970s and 1980s, with a top speed of 295 km/h.

- **The McLaren F1** can accelerate from 0-160 km/h in less time than it takes to read this sentence.

- **The McLaren F1** can go from 0 to 160 km/h and back to 0 again in under 20 seconds.

- **A tuned version** of the Chevrolet Corvette, the Callaway SledgeHammer, can hit over 400 km/h.

> ★ **STAR FACT** ★
> The Ford GT-90 has a top speed of 378 km/h and zooms from 0-100 km/h in 3.2 seconds.

A sailor's life

- **Sailors** used to be called 'tars' after the tarpaulins used for making sails. Tarpaulin is canvas and tar.

- **A sailor's duties** included climbing masts, rigging sails, taking turns on watch and swabbing (cleaning) decks.

- **The eight-hour** watches were timed with an hour glass.

- **Storing food** on ships in the days before canning was a problem. Sailors survived on biscuits and dried meat.

- **Hard tack** was hard biscuits that kept for years – but often became infested with maggots. The maggots were picked out before the biscuit was eaten.

- **Every sailor** had a daily ration of water of just over a litre since all water had to be carried on board.

- **Sailors** often made clothes from spare materials such as sail canvas.

- **Sailors who offended** against discipline might be flogged with a 'cat-o'-nine-tails' – a whip with nine lengths of knotted cord.

- **Sailors slept** in any corner they could find, often next to the cannon or in the darkness below decks.

- **Sailors' lavatories** on old ships were simply holes overhanging the sea called 'jardines', from the French for garden.

▼ *The introduction of the hammock in the 18th century made sleeping much less uncomfortable for sailors.*

Theatres

▶ There were several Wooden O theatres like this in Elizabethan London in the late 16th century – including the famous Globe where Shakespeare first staged his plays.

Entrance where the audience queued for the mid-afternoon performances

Walls made from plaster and wood

Rowdy audience pit where lower class stood

Bare stage where actors performed

Balconies where lords and ladies sat

- **In the days of Ancient Greece and Rome** thousands of people went to see dramas in huge, stone-built open-air theatres like sport arenas.

- **The Wooden Os** which appeared in England around 1570 were the first real theatres since Roman times. They were round wooden buildings with the stage and audience arena in the middle, open to the sky.

- **The 17th century** was the 'Golden Age' of drama in Spain, and people crammed into open courtyard theatres called corrales to see plays by great writers, such as Caldéron de la Barca and Lope de Vega.

- **In the 17th century** theatre moved indoors for the first time. Performances were by candlelight in large halls with rows of balconies round the edge.

- **In early theatres** the actors mostly performed on a bare stage. Towards the end of the 18th century, cut-out boards with realistic scenes painted on them were slid in from the wings (the sides of the stage).

- **In the early 19th century** theatres grew much bigger to cater for the populations of the new industrial cities, often holding thousands. Huge stages were illuminated by 'limelight' – brightly burning pellets of calcium.

- **Most of the grand old theatres** we can visit today date from the mid 19th century.

- **The big theatres** of the early 19th century had huge backstage areas with lots of room for 'flying in' scenery, and also spring loaded trapdoors and other ingenious mechanisms for creating giant special effects, like exploding volcanoes and runaway trains.

- **Towards the end of the 19th century** dedicated amateurs, fed up with special effects, performed in smaller spaces, such as clubs, barns and private houses. These developed into intimate 'studio' theatres where actors could stage subtle, realistic plays.

- **Many modern theatres** are equipped with very bright, computer-controlled lighting, sound systems and motorized stage machinery.

Submarines

- **The first workable submarine** was a rowing boat covered with waterproofed skins, built by Dutch scientist Cornelius Van Drebbel in 1620.

- **In 1776** David Bushnell's one-man sub USS *Turtle* attacked British ships in America's War of Independence.

- **Petrol engines** and electric batteries were combined to make the first successful subs in the 1890s.

- **Powerful,** less fumy diesel engines took over from 1908.

- **In 1954** the US launched the *Nautilus*, the first nuclear power sub. Now all subs are nuclear-powered.

- **U-boats** were German subs that attack Allied convoys of ships in World War I and II.

- **In a modern sub** a strong hull of steel or titanium stops it from being crushed by the pressure of water.

> ★ STAR FACT ★
> The tower on top of a submarine is called the sail or conning tower.

▶ To gain weight for a dive, submarines fill their 'ballast' tanks with water. To surface, they empty the tanks.

- **Most subs** are designed for war and have missiles called torpedoes to fire at enemy ships.

- **Attack** subs have guided missiles for attacking ships. Ballistic subs have missiles with nuclear warheads for firing at targets on land. The Russian navy has subs that can strike targets 8000 km away.

Model T Ford

- **In 1905** most cars were 'coach-built' which meant they were individually built by hand. This made them the costly toys of the rich only.

- **The dream of Detroit farmboy** Henry Ford was to make 'a motor car for the great multitude – a car so low in price that no man making a good fortune will be unable to own one.'

◀ The tough, cheap and reliable Model T – the first mass-produced car – put America on the road for the first time and earned the affection of two generations of American families.

- **Ford's solution** was to make a car, which he called the Model T, by the same mass production techniques also used to make guns at the time.

- **Mass production** meant using huge teams of men, each adding a small part to the car as it moved along the production line.

- **Body-panels** for the Model T were stamped out by machines, not hammered by hand as with earlier cars.

- **In 1908** when Ford launched the Model T, fewer than 200,000 people in the USA owned cars.

- **In 1913** 250,000 people owned Model Ts alone.

- **By 1930** 15 million Model Ts had been sold.

- **One of the keys to the T** was standardizations. Ford said early Ts were available in 'any colour they like so long as it's black.' Later models came in other colours.

- **The T's fragile-looking chassis** earned it the nickname 'Tin Lizzie', but it was made of tough vanadium steel.

Bridges of wood and stone

- **The first bridges** were probably logs and vines slung across rivers to help people across.
- **The oldest known bridge** was an arch bridge built in Babylon about 2200 BC.
- **Clapper bridges** are ancient bridges in which large stone slabs rest on piers (supports) of stone.
- **There are clapper bridges** in both Devon in England and Fujian in China.
- **The first brick bridges** were built by the Romans – like the Alcántara bridge over the Tagus River in Spain which was built around AD 100.
- **Long bridges** could be made with a series of arches linked together. Each arch is called a span.
- **Roman arches** were semi-circular, so each span was short; Chinese arches were flatter so they could span greater distances.
- **The Anji bridge** at Zhao Xian in China was built in AD 610 and it is still in use today.

▲ The Ponte Vecchio in Florence, built in 1345, is one of the oldest flattened arch bridges in Europe.

- **Flattened arched bridges** were first built in Europe in the 14th century. Now they are the norm.
- **London Bridge** was dismantled and reconstructed stone by stone in Arizona as a tourist attraction in 1971.

Autogiros and microlights

- **In the 1400s** many European children played with flying toys kept aloft by whirling blades.
- **The autogiro** was invented by the Spanish inventor Juan de la Cierva in 1923.
- **An autogiro** is lifted, not by wings, but by turning rotor blades.
- **A helicopter uses** a powerful motor to turn the rotors; an autogiro's rotors are turned round by the pressure of air as the plane flies forward.
- **The autogiro** is pulled forward by propeller blades on the front like an ordinary small plane.
- **The autogiro** can fly at up to 225 km/h, but cannot hover like a helicopter.
- **In the USA and Australia** microlights are called ultralights. They are small, very light aircraft.
- **The first microlight** was a hang-glider with a chainsaw motor, built by American hang-glider pioneer Bill Bennett in 1973.
- **Some microlights** have flexible fabric wings like hang-gliders.
- **Some microlights** have fixed wings with control flaps to steer them in flight.

◄ For a while in the 1930s, many people believed autogiros would be the Model T Fords of the air – aircraft for everyone.

Helicopters

Without a tail rotor, the helicopter would spin round the opposite way to the main rotors. This is called torque reaction. The tail rotor also acts as a rudder to swing the tail left or right

To fly up or down, the pilot alters the angle or 'pitch' of the main rotor blades with the 'collective pitch' control. When the blades cut through the air almost flat, they give no lift and the helicopter sinks. To climb, the pilot steepens the pitch to increase lift

Tail rotor drive shaft

To fly forwards or back, or for a banked turn, the pilot tilts the whole rotor with the 'cyclic pitch' control

The angle of the blades is changed via rods linked to a sliding collar round the rotor shaft, called the swashplate

Rockets

▶ A helicopter's rotor blades are really long, thin wings. The engine whirls them round so that they cut through the air and provide lift just like conventional wings (see taking off). But they are also like huge propellers, hauling the helicopter up just as a propeller pulls a plane.

Engine

Stabilizers

- **Toy helicopters** have been around for centuries, and those made by air pioneer Sir George Cayley in the early 19th century are the most famous.

- **On 13 November 1907** a primitive helicopter with two sets of rotors lifted French mechanic Paul Cornu off the ground for 20 seconds.

- **The problem** with pioneer helicopters was control. The key was to vary the pitch of the rotor blades.

- **In 1937** German designer Heinrich Focke built an aircraft with two huge variable pitch rotors instead of wings and achieved a controlled hover. Months later, German Anton Flettner built the first true helicopter.

- **Focke and Flettner's** machines had two rotors turning in opposite directions to prevent torque reaction. In 1939, Russian born American Igor Sikorsky solved the problem by adding a tail rotor.

- **The Jesus nut** that holds the main rotor to the shaft got its name because pilots said, "Oh Jesus, if that nut comes off...".

- **The biggest helicopter** was the Russian Mil Mi-12 Homer of 1968 which could lift 40,204 kg up to 2255 m.

- **The fastest helicopter** is the Westland Lynx, which flew at 402 km/h on 6 August 1986.

- **The Boeing/Sikorsky RAH-66** Comanche unveiled in 1999 is the first helicopter using stealth technology (see warplanes). It is made of carbon-fibre and other composite materials, and the rotor hub is hidden.

▲ The Vietnam war saw the rise of heavily armed helicopter gunships designed to hit targets such as tanks.

! NEWS FLASH !
The Bell Quad Tiltrotor has wings like a plane for fast flying. The propellers on the end of each wing tilt up in 20 seconds for vertical lift off. It could evacuate 100 people from danger in minutes.

Dams

▲ The gates of the Thames Barrier in London are designed to shut in times of very high tides to stop seawater flooding the city.

- **The earliest known dam** is a 15 m high brick dam on the Nile River at Kosheish in Egypt, built around 2900 BC.

- **Two Ancient Roman** brick dams, at Proserpina and Cornalbo in Southwest Spain, are still in use today.

- **In China** a stone dam was built on the Gukow in 240 BC.

- **Masonry dams** today are usually built of concrete blocks as gravity dams, arch dams or buttress dams.

- **Gravity dams** are very thick dams relying entirely on a huge weight of concrete to hold the water. They are very strong, but costly to build.

- **Arch dams** are built in narrow canyons and curve upstream. Buttress dams are thin dams strengthened by supports called buttresses on the downstream side.

- **Embankment dams** or fill dams are simple dams built from piles of earth, stones, gravel or clay.

- **The Aswan dam** on the Nile in Egypt has created Lake Nasser – one of the world's biggest artificial lakes.

- **The world's highest dams** are fill dams in Tajikistan – the Rogun (335 m) and Nurek (300 m). The highest gravity dam is the 285 m Grand Dixence in Switzerland. The highest arch dam is the 272 m Inguri in Georgia.

> ★ STAR FACT ★
> The world's biggest dam is the 255 m high, 112 million cu metre Kambaratinsk Dam in Russia.

Warships

- **21st-century navies** have five main classes of surface warship in descending size order: aircraft carriers, landing craft, cruisers, destroyers and frigates.

- **The biggest** warships are 332.9 m-long US aircraft carriers *Nimitz, Dwight D. Eisenhower, Carl Vinson, Abraham Lincoln, John C. Stennis, George Washington* and *Harry S. Truman.*

- **In World War II** cruisers had big guns and often acted independently; destroyers protected the main fleet; and frigates protected slower ships against submarines.

- **The distinction between** classes is now blurred. Cruisers are rare, and many small warships carry helicopters or even VTOL planes (see warplanes).

▶ A destroyer armed with a rotating gun for fleet escort.

- **The Russian** Moskva class are a cross between cruisers and aircraft carriers with rear flight decks for helicopters.

- **The British** Invincible class are small aircraft carriers able to carry six Harrier jump jets and twelve helicopters.

- **Warships** have largely replaced guns with missiles.

- **Warships** have both short-range missiles to fire against missiles and long-range supersonic missiles to fire against ships up to 500 km away.

- **The US Ticonderoga** ships are small cruisers built in the 1970s. They are powered by gas-turbine engines and armed with Tomahawk nuclear or conventional missiles.

- **The nuclear-powered** Russian Kirov class begun in 1973 are among the few big cruisers, over 22,000 tonnes.

Steam locomotives

- **Steam locomotives** get their power by burning coal in a firebox. This heats up water in a boiler, making steam. The steam drives a piston to and fro and the piston turns the wheels via connecting rods and cranks.

- **It takes about three hours** for the crew to get up enough steam to get a locomotive moving.

- **Coal and water** are often stored in a wagon called a tender, towed behind the locomotive.

- **A tender** holds 10 tonnes coal and 30,000 litres water.

- **One of the greatest 19th-century** loco designers was James Nasmyth.

- **A 4-6-2** has four small leading 'bogie' wheels, six big driving wheels and two small trailing wheels. The small bogie wheels carry much of the weight.

> ★ STAR FACT ★
> The first loco to hit 100 mph (160 km/h) was the City of Truro in 1895.

- **Loco classes** are described by their wheel layout.

- **In the American Civil War** (1861-65) *The General* was recaptured by Confederates after a chase in another loco.

- **The Flying Scotsman** was a famous loco designed by Sir Nigel Gresley (1876-1941). It pulled trains non-stop 630 km from London to Edinburgh in under six hours.

▼ *An American locomotive of the 1890s.*

Dhows

- **Dhows** are wooden Arab boats that have been used in the Mediterranean and Indian Ocean for thousands of years.

- **Most dhows** are now made of teak (or Glass Reinforced Plastic). In the past, mango wood was common.

- **In the past** dhows were made, not by nailing planks of wood together, but by sewing them with coconut fibre.

- **Dhow builders** rarely work from plans. They judge entirely by eye and experience.

- **Dhows traditionally** had lateen sails – triangular sails in line with the boat. This allows them to sail almost into the wind.

- **Although many dhows** are now motorized, they usually have a tall mast for unloading.

- **There are several kinds** of dhow, including the shu'ai, the boum, the sambuq, the jelbut and the ghanjah.

- **The jelbut** is thought to get its name from the English 'jolly boat' – the little boats visiting British East Indiamen sent ashore. Jelbuts were often used for pearl fishing. Racing jelbuts have a tree-trunk-like bowsprit almost as long as the hull to carry extra sails.

- **Sambuqs and ghanjahs** are thought to get their square sterns from 17th-century Portuguese galleons.

- **Boums** can be up to 400 tonnes and 50 m long.

▼ *Dhows like this are still built today in Lamu in Africa, much as they were 1000 or more years ago.*

Towns and cities

▲ The city of Florence is one of the most beautiful in the world. Many buildings date from the time when European towns began to flourish in the 15th century – especially in Italy.

- **The first cities** may date from the time when hunters and gatherers settled down to farm 10,000 years ago.
- **The city of Jericho** has been settled for over 10,000 years.
- **One of the oldest** known cities is Catal Hüyük in Anatolia in Turkey, dating from earlier than 6000 BC.
- **The first Chinese cities** developed around 1600 BC.
- **The cities of Ancient Greece** and Rome were often carefully laid out, with major public buildings. The first known town planner was the Ancient Greek Hippodamus, who planned the city of Miletus.
- **In the 1200s** Paris was by far the biggest city in Europe with a population of 150,000.
- **In the 1200s** 320,000 people lived in Hangzhou in China; Guangzhou (Canton) was home to 250,000.
- **In the 1400s** towns like Genoa, Bruges and Antwerp grew as trading centres. Medieval towns were rarely planned.
- **In the 1800s** huge industrial cities based on factories grew rapidly. Chicago's population jumped from 4000 in 1840 to 1 million in 1890.
- **The fastest growing** cities are places like Sao Paulo in Brazil where many poor people live in quickly erected shanty towns. The world's biggest city is Mexico City.

Luxury cars

- **The first Rolls-Royce** was made by Charles Rolls and Henry Royce. It was known as the 'best car in the world'.
- **The Rolls-Royce Silver Ghost** got its name for its ghost-like quietness and shiny aluminium body.
- **Today** each Rolls-Royce takes three months to build.
- **The winged girl** statuette on the bonnet of a Rolls-Royce is called 'Spirit of Ecstasy' and dates from 1911.
- **In the 1930s** Ettore Bugatti set out to build the best car ever with the Bugatti Royale. Only six were built, and they are now the world's most valuable cars.
- **The name Royale** comes from the King of Spain, Alfonso XIII, who was to buy the first model.
- **In 1925** drinksmaker André Dubonnet had a special version of the Hispano-Suiza H6B built with a body made entirely of tulipwood.
- **In the 1930s** American carmakers like Cord, Auburn and Packard made magnificent cars that Hollywood stars posed beside and Chicago gangsters drove.
- **Every 1934** Auburn speedster was sold with a plaque certifying it had been driven at over 100 mph (160 km/h) by racing driver Ab Jenkins.
- **The Mercedes in** Mercedes-Benz was the name of the daughter of Emil Jellinek, who sold the cars in the USA.

▶ Bentley is one of the great names in luxury cars. But founder Owen Bentley believed in racing as advertisement. The Bentley name gained lasting fame with success in the Le Mans 24-hour races of the 1920s. Seen here is a 1950s rally entry.

Towers

- **Romans, Byzantines** and medieval Europeans built towers in city walls and beside gates to give platforms for raining missiles on enemies.

- **Early churches** had square towers as landmarks to be seen from afar. From the 1100s, European cathedrals had towers called steeples, topped by a pointed spire.

- **Spires began** as pyramids on a tower, but got taller and were tapered to blend into the tower to make a steeple.

- **In the 17th and 18th centuries** church spires became simple and elegant, as in Park Street Church, Boston, USA.

- **The tallest unsupported tower** is Toronto's 553 m-high CN tower.

- **The tallest** tower supported by cables is the 629 m TV broadcast tower near Fargo and Blanchard in the USA.

- **The Tower of Babel** was a legendary tower built in ancient Babylon in the Near East. The Bible says God didn't want this high tower built, so he made the builders speak different languages to confuse them.

- **The Pharos** was a 135 m lighthouse built around 283 BC to guide ships into the harbour at Alexandria in Egypt.

- **The Tower of Winds,** or Horologium, was built in Athens around 100 BC to hold a sundial, weather vane and water clock.

- **Big Ben** is the bell in St Stephen's Tower in London's Houses of Parliament. The tower once had a cell where 'rioters' like suffragette Emmeline Pankhurst were held.

◀ *The Leaning Tower of Pisa in Italy is a 55 m high belltower or 'campanile'. Building began in 1173, and it started to lean as workers built the third storey. It is now 4.4 m out of true.*

The first houses

- **It was once thought** that all prehistoric humans lived in caves, but most caves were for religious rituals. The earliest houses were made of materials like wood, leaves, grass and mud – so traces have long since vanished.

- **Stone Age people** probably lived in round huts, with walls of wooden posts and thatches of reed.

- **In Britain** post holes and hearths have been found dating back 10,000 years in places like London's Hampstead Heath and Broom Hill in Hampshire.

- **Early mudbrick** houses dating from at least 9500 years ago are found in Anatolia in the Middle East.

- **Low walls** of big stones were the base for thatched roofs 6500 years ago at places like Carn Brea in Cornwall.

- **Two-storey houses** in Mohenjo Daro in Pakistan from 5000 years ago were built from sun-dried mud bricks and had courtyards, doors, windows and bathrooms.

- **Big Ancient Egyptian** houses had three main areas – a reception room for business, a hall in the centre for guests and private quarters at the back for family.

- **Tomb models** show what Egyptian homes were like.

- **Big Roman country houses** were called villas; a town house was called a domus.

- **Villas** had tiled roofs, verandahs, central heating, marbled floors, lavishly decorated walls and much more.

◀ *Some home-building styles have changed little in thousands of years. These houses are in French Polynesia.*

Record breaking cars

★ STAR FACT ★
On the 13 October 1997, a British jet car called *Thrust SSC* driven by British fighter pilot Andy Green broke the sound barrier for the first time. In two runs across Nevada's Black Rock desert it hit over 1220 km/h.

- **The first car speed record** was achieved by an electric Jentaud car in 1898 at Acheres near Paris. Driven by the Comte de Chasseloup-Laubat, the car hit 63.14 km/h. Camille Jenatzy vied with de Chasseloup-Laubat for the record, raising it to 105.85 km/h in his car *Jamais Contente* in 1899.

- **Daytona Beach** in Florida became a venue for speed trials in 1903. Alexander Winton reached 111 km/h in one of his Bullet cars.

- **The biggest engine** ever to be raced in a Grand Prix was the 19,891cc V4 of American Walter Christie, which he entered in the 1907 French Grand Prix. Later the Christie was the first front-wheel drive car to win a major race – a 400 km race on Daytona Beach.

- **The record** for the outer circuit at Brooklands in England was set in 1935 by John Cobb in a Napier-Railton at 1 min 0.41 sec (23,079 km/h) and never beaten.

▶ Donald Campbell took on the record-breaking mantle of his father –and the Bluebird name for his car. On 17 July 1964, Campbell's Bluebird hit a world record 690.909 km/h on the salt flats at Lake Eyre in South Australia. At one moment he hit over 716 km/h – faster than any wheel-driven car has ever been.

- In **1911** the governing body for the land speed record said that cars had to make two runs in opposite directions over a 1 km course to get the record.

- In **1924** Sir Malcolm Campbell broke the Land Speed Record for the first of many times in a Sunbeam at 235.17 km/h. In 1925 he hit 150 mph (242 km/h) for the first time. But his most famous record-breaking runs were in the 1930s in his own *Bluebirds*.

- In **1947** John Cobb drove with tremendous skill to reach 634.27 km/h in his Railton-Mobil. This stood as the record for 17 years.

- In **1964** the rules were changed to allow jet and rocket-propelled cars to challenge for the Land Speed Record. The next year Craig Breedlove drove his three-wheeler jet *Spirit of America* to over 500 mph (846.78 km/h).

- In **1970** Gary Gabelich set the record over 1000 km/h with his rocket-powered *Blue Flame*. This record wasn't beaten until Richard Noble roared to 1019.37 km/h in his Rolls-Royce jet-powered *Thrust 2* in 1983.

Bristol-Siddeley Proteus 705 gas-turbine engine pushing out 4500 horsepower

Drive shaft

Tail-plane for stability

Differential gear

Gas cylinders

Air intake

Exhaust ducts

Streamlined body shell for minimum drag

Solid rubber tyres

Tiny windscreen providing driver's only view

Lightweight aluminium wheels

Total weight of car is 4354 kg

Driver's cockpit

Ocean liners

▲ *One of the great transatlantic liners of the 1930s, the 'Queen Mary' (sister-ship of the 'Queen Elizabeth') is now a hotel at Long Beach California.*

- **The great age** of ocean liners lasted from the early 1900s to the 1950s.

- **Ocean liners** were huge boats, often with luxurious cabins, bars, games rooms and swimming pools.

- **The main route** was across the Atlantic. From 1833 liners competed for the Blue Riband title for fastest crossing.

- **Great Blue Riband** contenders included Brunel's *Great Western* in the 1830s, the *Mauretania* which held it from 1907 to 1929, and the French *Normandie* of the 1930s.

- **The last** ocean liner to hold the Blue Riband was the *United States* in the 1960s.

- **The famous Cunard line** was set up by Nova Scotia Quaker Samuel Cunard with George Burns and David MacIver in 1839.

- **The *Titanic*** was the largest ship ever built at 46,329 tonnes when launched in 1912 – but it sank on its maiden (first) voyage.

- **The sinking** of the liner *Lusitania* by a German submarine on 7 May 1915 with the loss of 1198 lives spurred the US to join the war against Germany.

- **The *Queen Elizabeth*** launched in 1938 was the largest passenger ship ever built – 314 m long and 83,673 tonnes. It burned and sank during refitting in Hong Kong in 1972.

- **Future liners** may be based on FastShip technology, with a very broad flat hull for high-speed stability.

The Tower of London

- **The Tower of London** is the oldest stone castle in London, started by William the Conqueror after his conquest of England in 1066. The Crown Jewels are kept here.

- **The oldest part of the tower** is the great square keep called the White Tower which dates from 1078.

- **The Tower** later gained two surrounding 'curtain' walls, like other castles.

- **The inner curtain** wall has 13 towers, including the Bloody Tower, Beauchamp Tower and Wakefield Tower.

- **Traitors' Gate** is an arch beside the River Thames. It gets its name from the time when high-ranking traitors were ferried here by boat to

▶ *The Tower of London is the most famous medieval castle in the UK.*

be imprisoned in the Tower. They entered this way.

- **Many people** have been imprisoned here like Princess (later Queen) Elizabeth and her mother Anne Boleyn (though not at the same time) in the 1500s.

- **Little Ease** is a dark 3.3 square metre cell where prisoners could neither stand up nor lie down.

- **Many prisoners were** beheaded, including Sir Thomas More and Sir Walter Raleigh.

- **In 1483** Edward V and his young brother were thought to have been murdered here. Bones which could have been theirs were later found under stairs.

- **Yeoman Warders** are the Tower's special guards. They are nicknamed beefeaters. The name may have come from a fondness for roast beef or the French word *buffetier*.

Greek and Roman building

▲ ▶ *The most famous Greek temple is the Parthenon in Athens, built c.450 BC.*

- **Ancient Greek and Roman** architecture are together known as Classical architecture.

- **The key features** of Classical buildings are solid, elegantly plain geometric shapes including pillars, arches and friezes.

- **The main Greek** building was the temple with its triangular roof of pale stone on rows of tall columns.

- **Greek temples** were designed in mathematical ratios.

- **Roman architect** Vitruvius described three orders (styles) of columns: Doric, Ionic and Corinthian.

- **Each order** has its own character: Doric serious and strong, Ionic graceful and Corinthian rich and festive.

- **The Parthenon** is a Doric temple built by architects Ictinus and Callicrates guided by the sculptor Phidias.

- **Roman buildings** used many arches and vaults (ceilings made from arches joined together).

- **The ruined Baths of Caracalla** in Rome (AD 217) has huge and graceful vaults.

- **Classical** architecture has inspired many imitations over the centuries, including the Palladian style of the 1600s.

Peoples' cars

- **The first car** for ordinary people was Ford's Model T. Ford built their ten millionth car in 1924 and their 50 millionth in 1959.

- **The USA** began making more than one million cars a year in 1916, of which over a third were Model Ts. No other country made a million cars a year until the UK in 1954.

- **Ford US** introduced weekly payment plans for new cars in 1923. The Nazis later borrowed the idea for the VW Beetle.

- **The Model A Ford** sold one million within 14 months of its launch in December 1927. The Ford Escort of 1980 sold a million in just 11 months.

- **The French Citroën 2CV** was designed to carry 'a farmer in a top hat across a ploughed field without breaking the eggs on the seat beside him'.

- **The VW Beetle** was the brain child of the Nazi dictator Adolf Hitler who wanted a cheap car for all Germans. It was created in 1938 by Ferdinand Porsche.

- **The war interrupted** VW Beetle production before it

had barely begun, but it was resumed after the war.

- **The ten millionth** VW Beetle was built in 1965. Over 22 million have now been sold.

- **The Soviet built Lada,** based on a design by Fiat, was one of the cheapest cars ever built.

- **The first British car** to sell a million was the Morris Minor, between 1949 and 1962.

▼ *The 1959 Mini, designed by Alec Issigonis set a trend in small car design, with the engine mounted across the car driving the front wheels.*

Bridges

▲ London's Tower Bridge was opened in 1894. It has a strong steel frame clothed in stone to support the two opening halves.

- **Rope suspension** bridges have been used for thousands of years. One of the first to use iron chains was the Lan Jin Bridge at Yunnan in China, built AD 65.

- **The first** all-iron bridge was at Coalbrookdale, England. It was designed by Thomas Pritchard and built in 1779 by Abraham Darby.

- **In the early 1800s** Thomas Telford began building superb iron bridges such as Craigellachie over the Spey in Scotland (1814). He built Europe's first iron chain suspension bridge over the Menai Straits in Wales in 1826.

- **Stephenson's** Britannia railway bridge of 1850, also over the Menai Straits, was the first hollow box girder bridge.

▶ Most bridges are now built of concrete and steel. Shown here are some of the main kinds. The longest are normally suspension bridges, usually carrying roads, but Hong Kong's 1377 m-long Tsing Ma (1998) takes both road and rail.

★ STAR FACT ★
The Akashi-Kaikyo Bridge (1998), Japan, is the world's longest suspension bridge with a main span of 1991 m and two side spans of 960 m.

- **John Roebling's** Cincinnati suspension bridge was the world's longest bridge when built in 1866 at 322 m. Like all suspension bridges today, it was held up by iron wires, not chains. It was the prototype for his Brooklyn Bridge.

- **The Forth Railway Bridge** in Scotland was the world's first big cantilevered bridge. At 520 m it was also the world's longest bridge when it was built in 1890.

- **In 1940** the Tacoma suspension bridge in Washington USA, was blown down by a moderate wind just months after its completion. The disaster forced engineers to make suspension bridges aerodynamic.

- **Aerodynamic design** played a major part in the design of Turkey's Bosphorus Bridge (1973) and England's Humber Bridge (1983), for a while the longest bridge at 1410 m.

- **In the 1970s** Japanese engineers began to build a bridge that by 2000 gave Japan nine of the world's 20 longest bridges.

In cable-stayed bridges, the bridge hangs directly from steel cables

In suspension bridges the bridge hangs on steel wires on a cable suspended between tall towers. They are light so can be very long

In cantilevered bridges, each half of the bridge is balanced on a support

Arch bridges are one of the oldest kinds and make very strong bridges

Bascule or lifting bridges like London's Tower Bridge swing up in the middle to allow tall ships through

Steel or concrete beam bridges are carried on piers. The beam may be a hollow steel girder through which cars and trains can run

The Statue of Liberty

- **New York's Statue of Liberty** stands on Liberty island off the tip of Manhattan.

- **The statue** was dedicated on 28 Oct 1886 by President Cleveland.

- **It was paid** for by the French people to celebrate their friendship with the USA.

- **Sculptor** Frédéric-Auguste Bartholdi began work on the statue in Paris in 1875.

◀ *New York's famous Statue of Liberty, before it was restored in 1986 and the flame covered in gold leaf.*

- **It was built** from 452 copper sheets hammered into shape by hand and mounted on four huge steel supports designed by Eiffel and Viollet-le-Duc.

- **The 225-tonne statue** was shipped to New York in 1885.

- **A pedestal** designed by Richard Hunt and paid for by 121,000 Americans brought it to a total height of 93 m.

- **The statue's** full name is *Liberty Enlightening the World*. The seven spikes in the crown stand for liberty's light shining on the world's seven seas and continents. The tablet in her left arm is America's Declaration of Independence.

- **Emma Lazarus's sonnet** *The New Colossus* on the pedestal ends: "Give me your tired poor, your huddled masses of your teeming shore. Send these, the homeless, tempest-tossed to me. I lift my lamp beside the golden door!"

> ★ **STAR FACT** ★
> The Statue of Liberty's crown houses an observation deck for up to 20 people.

Buses and coaches

- **Horse-drawn stage coaches** were the first regular public coach services between two or more points or 'stages'. They were first used in London in the 1630s.

- **Stage coaches** reached their heyday in the early 1800s when new tarred roads made travel faster. Coaches went from London to Edinburgh in 40 hours.

- **Bus is short** for 'omnibus' which in Latin means 'for all'. The word first came into use in Paris in the 1820s for big coaches carrying lots of people on local journeys.

- **In 1830** Goldsworthy Gurney put a steam engine in a coach to make the first powered bus. It ran four times a day between Cheltenham and Gloucester in England.

- **In the 1850s** British government laws restricted steam road vehicles, so big new cities developed horse buses.

- **In 1895** a petrol-engined bus was built in Germany.

- **In 1904** the London General Omnibus Co. ran the first petrol-engined bus services. They were double-decked.

- **1905:** the first motor buses ran on New York's 5th Avenue.

▲ *Like most early buses, this one from the early 1920s was built by adding a coach body to a lorry base.*

- **1928:** the first transcontinental bus service crossed the USA.

- **From the 1950s** articulated buses were used in European cities. A trailer joined to the bus carries extra passengers.

St Basil's cathedral

- **The cathedral of** St Basil the Blessed in Moscow's Red Square was built from 1554 to 1560.

- **St Basil's** is made up of ten tower churches, the biggest of which is 46 m tall.

- **It began with** eight little wooden churches – each built between 1552 and 1554 after a major Russian victory against the Tartars of Kazan in central Asia.

- **After the final victory**, Ivan the Terrible ordered stone churches to be built in place of the wooden ones.

- **Legend says** each of the onion-shaped domes represents the turban of a defeated Tartar lord.

▲ With its ten famous colourful towers, St Basil's in Moscow one of the most beautiful Christian cathedrals in the world.

- **St Basil's** was designed by two Russians, Posnik and Barma, who may have been one person.

- **Legend says** the Italian builder was blinded afterwards so he could build nothing like it again.

- **Originally** it was known as the Cathedral of the Intercession, but in 1588 a tenth church was added in honour of St Basil and it was known afterwards as St Basil's.

- **St Basil** was the jester (comedian) to a Moscow lord of the time.

- **In 1955**, restorers found the secret of the cathedral's construction embedded in the brickwork – wooden models used as silhouettes to guide the builders.

Hydrofoils

- **Hydrofoils** are boats with hulls that lift up above the water when travelling at high speeds.

- **The hydrofoils** are wings attached to the hull by struts that move underwater like aeroplane wings and lift the boat up.

- **Because only the foils** dip in the water, hydrofoils avoid water resistance, so can travel faster with less power.

- **Surface-piercing hydrofoils** are used in calm inland waters and skim across the surface.

▼ By lifting themselves out of the water and almost flying across the surface, hydrofoils achieve very high speeds.

> ★ **STAR FACT** ★
> The biggest hydrofoil, built in Seattle, is the 64 m long, 92 km/h *Plainview* navy transport.

- **Full-submerged hydrofoils** dip deep into the water for stability in seagoing boats.

- **The foils** are usually in two sets, bow and stern.

- **The bow and stern foils** are in one of three arrangements. 'Canard' means the stern foil is bigger. 'Airplane' means the bow foil is bigger. 'Tandem' means they are both the same size.

- **The first successful hydrofoil** was built by Italian Enrico Forlanini in 1906.

- **In 1918** Alexander Graham Bell, inventor of the telephone, built a hydrofoil that set a world water speed record at 61.6 knots (114 km/h). The record was not beaten until the American *Fresh 1*, another hydrofoil, set a new record of 84 knots (155 km/h) in 1963.

Balloons

- **Balloons** are bags filled with a light gas or hot air – both so light that the balloon floats in the air.
- **Balloons** designed to carry people into the air are of two types: hot-air balloons and gas balloons filled with hydrogen or helium.
- **Hot-air balloons** have a burner that continually fills the balloon with warm air to keep it afloat.
- **To carry two people** a hot-air balloon must have a bag of about 1700 cubic metres in volume.
- **Balloons** are normally launched at dusk or dawn when the air is quite calm.
- **As the air in the bag cools**, the balloon gradually sinks. To maintain height, the balloonist lights the burner to add warm air again.
- **To descend quickly** the balloonist pulls a cord to let air out through a vent in the top of the bag.
- **The first flight** in a hot air balloon was made in Paris on 15 October 1783 by French scientist Jean de Rozier in a

▶ Hot air ballooning has become a popular sport since Ed Yost, Tracy Barnes and other Americans began to make the bags from polyester in the 1960s.

balloon made by the Montgolfier brothers.
- **The first hydrogen gas balloon flight** was made in Paris on 1 December 1783.
- **On 20 March 1999** Swiss Bertran Piccard and British Brian Jones made the first round-the-world hot air balloon flight.

Record breaking flights

- **On 25 July 1909** Louis Blériot made the first flight across the English Channel in a plane he built himself.
- **In May 1919** Capt A.C. Read and his crew made the first flight across the Atlantic in a Curtiss flying boat.
- **On 14-15 June 1919** John Alcock and Arthur Brown made the first non-stop flight across the Atlantic in an open cockpit Vickers Vimy biplane.

★ STAR FACT ★
In December 1986, *Voyager*, piloted by Rutan and Yeager, flew non-stop round the world in 9 days.

- **In November 1921** brothers Keith and Ross Smith made the first flight from England to Australia.
- **On 4 May 1924** Frenchman Étienne Oehmichen flew his helicopter in a 1 km circle.
- **In 1927** Frenchman Louis Breguet made the first flight across the South Atlantic.
- **On 21 May 1927** American Charles Lindbergh made the first solo flight across the Atlantic in the *Spirit of St Louis*.
- **In July 1933** Wiley Post made the first solo round-the-world flight.
- **The story of Post's epic** flight was told in the book *Round the World in Eight Days*.

◀ Blériot being greeted near Dover after completing his flight across the English channel.

St Paul's cathedral

- **The current St Paul's** cathedral in London is the fifth church on the site.

- **On the same site** in Roman times, there was a temple dedicated to Diana.

- **The first St Paul's** was built of wood in AD 604 by St Ethelbert, King of Kent.

- **The Norman cathedral** was started around 1090 by Maurice, chaplain to William the Conqueror.

- **The Norman cathedral** called 'Old St Paul's' had the highest spire ever built, but it was struck down by lightning in 1561.

- **The first public lottery** was held in Old St Paul's in 1569 to raise money for repairs. The churchyard was famous for its booksellers, like Wynkyn de Worde in the 1400s.

◄ St Paul's is one of the world's largest and most elegant cathedrals. It was built in the classical (Roman) style by the great architect Christopher Wren in the 17th century.

- **Old St Paul's** burned to the ground in the Great Fire of London in 1666.

- **The new St Paul's** was designed by Sir Christopher Wren, who designed many other London buildings. Wren thought the 111 m-high dome he wanted to be seen from the outside was too lofty for the inside. So inside the outer dome, he built another 20 m lower. Work began in 1675 and was completed in 1711.

- **If you whisper** inside the dome's famous 'whispering gallery' you can be heard on the far side 35 m away.

- **Among the famous tombs** in the crypt of St Paul's are those of Admiral Nelson and the Duke of Wellington.

Boat building

◄ Building boats in wood is a tremendously skilled craft that dates back many thousands of years.

- **For much of history** ships were built and designed by shipwrights.

- **Shipwrights** worked from experience and rarely drew plans. But in the 17th and 18th centuries, they often made models.

- **Nowadays** ships are designed by 'naval architects' and built by shipbuilders.

> **★ STAR FACT ★**
> A futtock is one of the big bent timber ribs of a boat near the stern.

- **Wooden ships** were put together on a building berth. Timbers and planks were cut and shaped around, then fitted together on the berth to form the ship's hull.

- **First the long spine** or keel of the boat was laid down. Thick wooden ribs were added to make a strong frame.

- **In the Middle Ages** in the Mediterranean, wooden ships were carvel-built. This means the planks were fitted together edge to edge onto the ribs.

- **In the Middle Ages** in northern Europe, wooden ships were clinker-built. This means the planks overlapped, as in Viking ships.

- **Ships** are launched down a slope called a slipway.

- **After launching** a ship has just the bare bones of a hull and main structures. It is finished in a fitting-out basin.

Hovercraft

- **A hovercraft** or air cushion vehicle floats on a layer of compressed air just above the ground. It is also called a ground-effect machine. The air means there is very little friction between the craft and the ground.

- **A hovercraft** has one or more big fans that suck air into the craft, then blow it down underneath. The air is trapped underneath by a flexible rubber skirt.

- **The idea began with** Sir John Thornycroft in the 1870s. He thought drag on a ship's hull could be reduced if an indent in the hull allowed it to ride on a cushion of air. But for decades no-one could work out how to contain the air.

- **In the 1950s** Christopher Cockerell cracked the problem by pumping air down around the edge of a curtain-like skirt. The air itself then sealed the cushion of air inside the curtain.

- **In 1959** the world's first practical hovercraft, the SRN1 was built, using Cockerell's system. It crossed the English Channel on the 50th anniversary of Blériot's first flight across the channel.

- **In the late 1960s** the US Army and navy began using hovercraft in the Vietnam war for patrol and rescue missions because of their ability to go over land, water and swampy ground equally easily. The Russian and US armies are still the biggest users of hovercraft.

- **In 1968** big hovercraft able to carry scores of cars and lorries were introduced as ferries across the English Channel, but elsewhere they have not lived up to expectations. The biggest cross-Channel hovercraft was the 56 m-long SRN4 MkIII which carried 418 passengers and 60 cars at speeds over 120 km/h.

- **In the late 1950s** French engineer Jean Bertin developed a train called a tracked air cushion vehicle or TACV. This is basically a hovercraft on rails. Trains like this could swish between cities almost silently at speeds of 500 km/h.

- **On 25 January 1980** a 100-tonne US Navy hovercraft, the SES 100-B, reached a record speed of 170 km/h – faster than any warship has ever travelled.

▼ *Hovercraft vary in speed, size and power, but they are used essentially for one of two purposes – as ferries across short stretches of water, like this one, or by the army and navy. In smaller hovercraft, the fan that forces the air into the cushion is often the same one that drives the craft forward. In bigger ones like this, there are separate driving propellers mounted on the back, working in much the same way as aircraft propellers to drive the craft along.*

> **! NEWS FLASH !**
> Hospitals can use special hoverbeds to support badly burned patients on air.

Rubberized bag skirt, holding the air cushion in

Flight deck

Powerful gas turbine for the lifting fan

Passenger compartment in which people travel as they would on an aeroplane. There is no deck as on a conventional boat

Double propellers for driving the hovercraft forwards or backwards at speeds of up to 120 km/h

Rudders to steer the craft. These become more effective the faster the hovercraft is travelling

Chinese building

- **China** developed its own distinctive style of building over 3000 years ago.

- **Traditionally, large Chinese buildings** were made of wood on a stone base.

- **A distinctive feature** is a large tiled overhanging roof, ending in a graceful upturn. The tiles were glazed blue, green or yellow.

- **The roof** is supported not by the walls but by wooden columns, often carved and painted red and gold.

- **Walls were thin** and simply gave privacy and warmth.

- **Chinese temples** were large wooden halls with elaborate roof beams in the ceiling.

- **Pagodas** are tall tapering towers often linked to Buddhist temples. They have from 3 to 15 storeys.

> ★ STAR FACT ★
> Chinese pagodas have eight sides and an uneven number of storeys.

▲ The Forbidden City in Beijing dates mostly from the Ming era from 1368-1644. Only the emperor's household could enter it.

- **In China, pagodas** were believed to bring happiness to the surrounding community. They were made of wood, bricks, tiles or even porcelain and decorated with ivory.

- **Pagodas**, originally from India, developed from Buddhist burial mounds called stupas.

Canoes

- **The first canoes** were scooped out logs.

- **A skin canoe** was made by stretching animal skins over a bent wood frame.

- **A skin canoe** dating from around 4500 BC was found on the Baltic island of Fünen.

◀ ▼ The materials may be different, but today's bright fibreglass canoes are based on the same principles as the ancient bark canoes of native Americans.

- **Some skin canoes** are round like the paracil and the Welsh coracle.

- **Some skin canoes** are long and thin like the Irish curach and the Inuit kayak.

- **Kayaks** have a watertight cover made from sealskin to keep out water in rough conditions.

- **The ancient quffa** of Iraq is a large canoe made of basketwork sealed with tar and dates back to 4000 BC.

- **Native Americans** made canoes from bark. The Algonquins used paper birch, the Iroquois elm.

- **Bark canoes** were the basis for today's sport canoes of fibreglass, plastic and aluminium.

- **Unlike ordinary boats,** canoes are often so light that they can easily be carried overland to avoid waterfalls or to move from one river to another.

Electric trains

- **The first practical** electric trains date from 1879, but they only became widespread in the 1920s.

- **Electric locos** pick up electric current either from a third 'live' rail or from overhead cables.

- **To pick up** power from overhead cables, locos need a spring-loaded frame or pantograph to conduct electricity to the transformer.

- **Electric trains** are clean and powerful, and can also travel faster than other trains.

- **Older systems** mostly used Direct Current (DC) motors, operating at 1500-3000 volts for overhead cables and 700 volts for live rails.

- **High-speed trains** like France's TGV and Japan's Shinkansen use 'three-phase' Alternating Current (AC) motors operating at 25,000 volts.

◀ *Japan's Shinkansen 'bullet train' was the first of the modern high speed electric trains, regularly operating at speeds of over 400 km/h.*

- **The Paris-London Eurostar** works on 25,000 volt AC overhead cables in France, and 750 volt live rails after it comes out of the Channel Tunnel in England.

- **Magnetic levitation** or maglev trains do not have wheels but glide along supported by electromagnets.

- **In electrodynamic maglevs**, the train rides on repulsing magnets. In electromagnetic maglevs, they hang from attracting magnets.

- **Maglevs** are used now only for short, low-speed trains, but they may one day be the fastest of all. High-speed maglev developments now use 'superconducting' electromagnets which are costly to make. But a new idea is to use long strings of ordinary permanent magnets.

Stations

- **London Bridge** station is the oldest big city terminal, first built from wood in 1836, then of brick in the 1840s.

- **In the 19th century** railway companies competed to make the grandest, most palatial railway stations.

- **The Gare d'Orsay** in Paris was an incredibly luxurious station built in 1900 in what is called the *Beaux Arts* (beautiful arts) style. It is now a museum and gallery.

- **When first built** in 1890, Sirkeci in Istanbul – terminal of the Orient Express – glittered like an oriental palace.

- **Bombay's Victoria** – now Chhatrapati Sivaji – was built in 1888 over a shrine to Mumba Devi, named after the patron goddess of original inhabitants of Bombay.

- **Grand Central Station** in New York cost a staggering 43 million dollars to build in 1914.

- **Liverpool Street Station** in London was built in 1874 on the site of the 13th century Bedlam hospital for lunatics.

- **London's St Pancras** is a stunning Gothic building designed by George Gilbert Scott. It was built 1863-72.

- **Chicago's** North Western is a monument to the Jazz Age in the city, dating from 1911.

- **In April 1917** Lenin returned to Russia and announced the start of the Russian revolution at St Petersburg's famous Finland Railway station.

▼ *The great hall at Grand Central Station in New York is one of the most spectacular railway halls in the world.*

Submersibles

- **Submersibles** are small underwater craft. Some are designed for very deep descents for ocean research. Others are designed for exploring wrecks.

- **One early submersible** was a strong metal ball or bathysphere, lowered by cables from a ship.

- **The bathysphere** was built by Americans William Beebe and Otis Barton who went down 900 m in it off Bermuda on 11 June 1931. The possibility of the cable snapping meant the bathysphere was very dangerous.

- **The bathyscaphe** was a diving craft that could be controlled underwater, unlike the bathysphere. Its strong steel hull meant it could descend 4000 m or more.

- **The first bathyscaphe**, the FNRS 2, was developed by Swiss scientist August Piccard between 1946 and 1948. An improved version, the FNRS 3, descended 4000 m off Senegal on 15 February 1954. The FNRS 3 was further improved to make the record-breaking *Trieste*.

- **In the 1960s** the Woods Hole Oceanographic Institute in the USA began to develop a smaller, more manoeuvrable submersible, called *Alvin*. *Alvin* is one of the most famous of all submersibles, making thousands of dives to reveal a huge amount about the ocean depths.

- **ROVs** or Remote Operated Vehicles are small robot submersibles. ROVs are controlled from a ship with video cameras and computer virtual reality systems. ROVs can stay down for days while experts are called in to view results. Using the ROV Argo-Jason, Robert Ballard found the wreck of the liner *Titanic* in 1985.

- ***Deep Flight*** is a revolutionary submersible with wings that can fly underwater like an aeroplane, turning, diving, banking and rolling.

- **A new breed** of small submersibles, like the *Sea Star* and *Deep Rover*, cost about the same as a big car and are designed for sports as well as research.

▶ This is one of the first of the huge range of submersibles that began to appear in the 1960s and 70s. They are now much smaller, neater and more manoeuvrable, but still work in much the same way.

Searchlights for seeing the dark ocean depths

Entry hatch

Claw for grabbing samples

Double hatch containing airlock for divers to go out

Cabin of strong steel to resist intense water pressure

Powerful electric motor

Propeller for pushing the craft through the water

To go back up to the surface, the pilot switches off the electromagnets that hold the ballast of iron balls in place

Batteries

Video camera

Extra strong perspex dome

As the craft descends, the petrol is compressed and gives less buoyancy, speeding the descent

Float filled with petrol. Since petrol is lighter than water, it helps keep the craft afloat

★ STAR FACT ★
On 23 January 1960, the bathyscaphe *Trieste*, controlled by August Piccard's son Jacques, descended a record 10,916 m in the Marianas Trench in the Pacific.

Airports

- **The world's first airport** was built at Croydon near London in 1928. Many early airports, like Berlin's, were social centres attracting thousands of visitors.

- **Before airports,** flying boats would land on water. So airports like New York's La Guardia were set close to water to take flying boats.

- **Over 50 airports** around the world now handle over 10 million passengers a year. 25 of these are in the USA.

- **Six airports** handle over 30 million passengers, including Chicago's O'Hare and Hong Kong's Chep Lap Kok.

- **The world's largest** airport is King Abdul Aziz in Saudi Arabia. It covers 22,464 hectares. The USA's biggest is Dallas. Europe's biggest is Paris's Charles de Gaulle.

- **Hong Kong's** Chep Lap Kok airport, opened in 1998, is one of the world's most modern.

- **Kansai** airport in Japan is built entirely on an artificial island in Osaka Bay so that it can operate 24-hours a day, without disturbing people with noise.

▲ In the 1970s, Boeing 747 jumbo jets needed 4 km runways to take-off, but better performance means they now need less distance.

- **In early airports** terminals for each flight were set in a line as at Kansas and Munich. But as flights increased, this layout meant passengers had a long way to walk.

- **Terminals in the 1970s** were set in extending piers like Amsterdam's Schiphol, or satellites like Los Angeles.

- **New airport terminals** like London's Stansted are set apart and linked by electric cars called 'people-movers'.

Trams and cable cars

- **Trams** are buses that run on rails laid through city streets. They are called streetcars in the USA.

- **Early trams** in the 1830s were pulled by horses. By the 1870s, horse-drawn trams were used in many cities.

- **In 1834** Thomas Davenport, a blacksmith from Vermont, USA built a battery-powered electric tram.

- **In 1860** an American called George Train set up battery-powered electric tram systems in London.

- **In 1873** Andrew Hallidie introduced cable cars in San Francisco. The cars were hauled by a cable running in a slot in the street. A powerhouse pulled the cable at around 14 km/h. Similar systems were built in many cities in the 1880s but were soon replaced by electric trams.

- **In 1888** Frank Sprague demonstrated a tram run from electric overhead cables in Richmond in the USA.

- **In most US trams,** electric current was picked up via a long pole with a small wheel called a shoe that slid along the cable. The pick-up was called a trolley.

Many European trams, however, picked up current via a collapsible frame called a pantograph.

- **In the early 1900s,** electric tram systems were set up in most world cities.

- **In the 1930s** most cities, except in eastern Europe and Russia, replaced trams with buses.

- **In the 1990s** some cities, like Manchester in England, built new tramways, because they are fume-free.

◄ The original Hallidie cable car system dating from 1873 still runs in San Francisco.

The Wright brothers

- **The Wright brothers,** Orville and Wilbur, built the world's first successful plane, the *Flyer*.

- **On 17 December 1903** the Wright brothers made the first powered, long and controlled airplane flight at Kitty Hawk, USA.

◀ *One of the five who witnessed the flight took this picture. But apart from a report in 'Popular Science' the Wrights' success was little known about for five years.*

- **Wilbur Wright** was born in 1867 on a farm near New Castle, Indiana; Orville was born in 1871 in Dayton, Ohio.

- **The Wright brothers** began as bicycle makers but became keen on flying after hearing about the death of pioneer glider Otto Lilienthal in 1896.

- **From 1899 to 1903** they worked at Kitty Hawk methodically improving their design and flying skill.

- **Many early planes** took off but lacked control. The key to the Wrights' success was stopping the plane rolling, using wires to 'warp' (twist) the wings to lift one side or the other.

- **The *Flyer*'s** wing warp meant it could not only fly level but make balanced, banked turns (like a bicycle cornering).

- **For the first flight** Orville was at the controls.

- **The historic first flight** lasted 12 seconds, in which the *Flyer* travelled 37 m and landed safely.

- **On 5 October 1905** the Wrights flew 38.9 km in 38 mins.

Bicycles

▲ *Bicycles are the cheapest, most reliable form of transport ever, and in the 1920s many tradesmen adapted them for use.*

- **The first bicycle** was the 'draisienne' of 1818 of Baron de Drais. The rider scooted his feet on the ground to move.

- **In 1839** Scots blacksmith Kirkpatrick Macmillan invented the first bicycle with pedals and brakes.

- **On Macmillan's 'velocipede'** pedals were linked by rods to cranks on the back wheel. These turned the wheel slowly.

- **In 1861** French father and son Pierre and Ernest Michaux stuck the pedals directly on the front wheel to make the first successful bicycle, nicknamed 'boneshaker'.

- **In 1870** James Starley improved the boneshaker with the Ordinary. A huge front wheel gave high speed with little pedalling.

- **In 1874** H. J. Lawson made the first chain-driven bicycle. This was called a 'safety bicycle' because it was safer than the tall Ordinary.

- **In 1885** Starley's nephew John made the Rover Safety bicycle. Air-filled tyres were added in 1890, and the modern bicycle was born.

- **By 1895** four million Americans were riding bicycles.

- **Today** 50 million people in the USA cycle regularly.

- **More people** in China cycle today than the rest of the world put together.

Great voyages

▶ In 1580, Sir Francis Drake became the first Englishman to sail round the world. En route, he visited what is now California.

● **In 330 BC** the Greek sailor Pytheas sailed out into the Atlantic through the Straits of Gibraltar and found his way to 'Thule' (Britain).

● **Around AD 1000** the Viking Leif Ericsson was the first European to cross the Atlantic to North America.

● **In 1405** Chinese admiral Cheng Ho began a series of seven epic voyages around the Indian Ocean in a huge fleet of junks.

● **In 1492** Genoese Christopher Columbus crossed the Atlantic from Cadiz in Spain and discovered the New World. His ship was the *Santa Maria*.

> ★ STAR FACT ★
> In 1522, Ferdinand Magellan's ship *Victoria* completed the first round-the-world voyage.

● **From 1499-1504** Italian Amerigo Vespucci sailed the Atlantic and realized South America was a continent. America is named after him.

● **In 1492** Italian John Cabot crossed the North Atlantic from Bristol in England and found Canada.

● **In 1498** Portuguese Vasco da Gama was the first European to reach India by sea, sailing all round Africa.

● **In 1642** Dutchman Abel Tasman sailed to what is now Australia and New Zealand. The island of Tasmania is named after him.

● **From 1768-79** James Cook explored the South Pacific in his ship the *Endeavour* and landed at Botany Bay.

▶ Like many 15th century explorers, Columbus sailed a 'carrack' with 'lateen' sails for sailing close in to the wind.

Ancient palaces

● **The word palace** comes from the Palatine Hill in Rome, where the emperors of Rome had their palaces.

● **The earliest known** palaces are those built in Thebes in Ancient Egypt by King Thutmose III in the 15th century BC.

● **Egyptian palaces** had a rectangular wall enclosing a maze of small rooms and a courtyard – a pattern later followed by many Asian palaces.

● **The Babylonians** and Persians introduced grand halls in their palaces at Susa and elsewhere.

● **Minoan palaces** on Crete introduced extra storeys.

● **Roman palaces** were the grandest of the ancient world.

● **The Sacred Palace** of Byzantium (now Istanbul) was biggest of all, covering 334,000 square metres.

● **Palaces** in China and Japan, like Beijing's Forbidden City, often had a high wall surrounding small houses for the ruler and his officials.

● **Ancient palaces in the Americas** like the Mayan palace at Uxmal dating from AD 900, are usually simpler.

● **Potala palace** stands high above Lhasa in Tibet. Potala means 'high heavenly realm'. The original, built by King Srong-brtsan-sgam-po in the 7th century was destroyed by the Chinese c.1600. The Dalai Lama rebuilt it in 1645.

◀ The 12th-century Khmer emperors of Cambodia built magnificent palaces in their capital of Angkor, now overgrown by jungle. But most magnificent of all was the temple, Angkor Wat.

Docks and ports

- **Some ports** like Hong Kong and Rio, are based on natural harbours; others are constructed artificially.

- **The Phoenicians** built artificial harbours at Tyre and Sidon in the Lebanon in the 13th-century.

- **The Romans** invented waterproof concrete to build the quays and breakwaters at their port of Ostia.

- **Roman and other ancient ports** had animal and human powered cranes. Saxon London and Viking Dublin had well-built wooden wharves.

- **Traditionally,** big boats would anchor in mid stream and barges called lighters would take the cargo ashore.

- **In the 18th-century** the first enclosed deep water docks were built at London and Liverpool. Here big ships could moor and unload directly onto the wharves.

> ★ STAR FACT ★
> The world's busiest ports are Rotterdam, Singapore and Hong Kong.

- **In the 20th century,** ports specializing in particular cargoes, such as oil terminals, grew.

- **Since the 1950s** there has been a huge growth in container ports. Containers are big standardized metal crates that can be loaded on and off quickly.

- **The world's main container ports** are Hong Kong, Singapore, Rotterdam, Hamburg and New York.

▲ *The port of Balstad in Norway, a perfect natural harbour.*

Modern architecture

▶ *The old and new in Hong Kong: the ultra modern Hong Kong-Shanghai bank dwarfs a 19th-century classical building.*

- **In the 1920s** many architects rejected old styles to experiment with simple shapes in materials like glass, steel and concrete.

- **The International Style** was pioneered by architect Le Corbusier who built houses in smooth geometric shapes like boxes.

- **The Bauhaus** school in Germany believed buildings should look like the job they were meant to do.

- **Walter Gropius** and Mies van de Rohe took Bauhaus ideas to the US and developed sleek, glass-walled, steel-framed skyscrapers like New York's Seagram Building.

- **American Frank Lloyd Wright** (1869-1959) was famous both for his low, prairie-style bungalows 'growing' from their site and his airy and elegant geometric buildings.

- **In the 1950s** architects like Kenzo Tange of Japan reacted against the 'blandness' of the International Style, introducing a rough concrete look called Brutalism.

- **In the 1960s** many critics reacted against the damage done by modern architecture to historic cities.

- **Post-modernists** were united in rejecting modern architecture, often reviving historical styles. American Robert Venturi added traditional decoration.

- **Richard Rogers'** Pompadou centre in Paris (1977) was a humorous joke on the Bauhaus idea, exposing the 'bones' of the building.

- **With shiny metal** and varied shapes the Guggenheim gallery in Bilbao in Spain is a new masterpiece.

Pyramids

- **Pyramids** are huge ancient monuments with a square base and triangular sides coming together in a point at the top. Remarkably, they are found not only in Egypt, but also in Greece, Cyprus, Italy, India, Thailand, Mexico, South America and various Pacific islands.

- **The earliest tombs** of the pharaohs were mud chambers called mastabas. But c.2686 BC, the wise man Imhotep had a pyramid-shaped tomb built for Zoser at Saqqara. This rose in steps and so is called the Step Pyramid.

- **In 2600BC** the Egyptians filled in the steps on a pyramid with stones to make the first smooth pyramid at Medum.

- **The ruins of 80 pyramids** stand near the Nile in Egypt, built over 1000 years. Each has an elaborate system of hidden passageways and chambers to stop robbers getting at the tomb of the pharaoh inside.

- **The largest pyramid** is the Great Pyramid at Giza, built for the Pharaoh Khufu c.2551-2472 BC. This was once 147 m high, but is now 140 m, since some upper stones have been lost. Khufu is known as Cheops in Greek.

▶ The strange half lion, half pharaoh statue called the Sphinx stands near the pyramid of pharaoh Khafre at Giza.

- **Later,** the Egyptians abandoned pyramids and cut tombs into rock, as in the Valley of Kings at Thebes. The tomb of Tutankhamun was one of these.

- **The Moche Indians** of Peru built large brick pyramids, including the Pyramid of the Sun near Trujillo.

- **Another Pyramid of the Sun** is on the site of the ancient Aztec capital of Teotihuacan, 50 km from Mexico City. Built around 2000 years ago it is exactly the same size (230 m square) as the Great Pyramid at Giza.

- **The American pyramids** were not tombs like those in Egypt, but temples, so they have no hidden chambers inside. They are built not from blocks of cut stone but from millions of basketloads of volcanic ash and gravel.

> ★ STAR FACT ★
> The Great Pyramid at Giza was made of 2.3 million 2.5 tonne blocks of limestone.

▶ No-one knows just how the Egyptians managed to build such huge structures as the pyramids. It is thought that over 100,000 people worked on each big pyramid. Each big block was probably cut from the quarry, dragged on rollers to the River Nile and carried on barge to the building site. The stones were then dragged into place up earth ramps.

Underground Chamber

King's Chamber

Grand Gallery

Queen's Chamber

Funeral temple

Mastaba tombs

Boat pit

The Queen's Pyramids

Moving on snow

▲ *Cutters are still used in the north eastern USA as a charming way of getting around in the winter snows.*

- **Vehicles** designed to move on snow are supported on flat boards called runners, skids or skis. These slide over snow easily and spread the vehicle's weight over a larger area.

- **Sleds or sleighs** drawn by horses or dogs may have been the first vehicles ever used by humans.

- **Cutters** are light, graceful horse-drawn sleighs first introduced in the USA about 1800.

- **Troikas** are Russian sleighs (or carriages) drawn by three horses. The middle horse is supposed to trot while the outer horses gallop in particular ways.

- **Native Americans** had toboggans made of poles tied with leather thongs.

- **Snowmobiles** are vehicles with two skis at the front and a motor-driven track roll at the back. Racing snowmobiles can reach over 160 km/h.

- **Snowmobiles** are steered by handlebars that control the skis and by the shifting of the driver's weight.

- **The first propeller-driven** snowmobile was built in the 1920s. Tracked snowmobiles were developed in 1959 by Canadian Joseph Bombardier.

- **In the 1960s,** carved wooden skis dating back 8000 years were found in a bog at Vis near the Urals in Russia.

- **The earliest skates** were made from small bones.

Rescue boats

- **Several designs** for 'unsinkable' lifeboats were tried in 18th-century France and England.

- **After many drowned** when the ship *Adventure* went down in 1789, a competition for a lifeboat was set up.

- **The competition winner** was Newcastle boatbuilder Henry Greathead. His boat the *Original* would right itself when capsized and still float even when nearly filled with water.

- **The first land-based** powered lifeboat was steam powered and launched in 1890.

- **Around 1907** diesel-power lifeboats were introduced. Without the need for oars, most

- of the boat could be covered in and so made even more unsinkable.

- **Modern land-based lifeboats** are either steel-hulled or made of a double-skin of timber.

- **The hull** usually contains a large number of sealed air containers so it is almost impossible for the boat to sink.

- **Some lifeboats** are afloat all the time. Others are kept ashore in a lifeboat house ready for emergencies.

- **Lifeboats** kept ashore are launched down a slipway into the sea or wheeled into the sea on a cradle until they float.

- **As leisure sailing** and bathing has increased, so there has been an increase in the number of inshore rescue boats. These are small rubber or fibreglass boats, kept afloat by an inflatable tube of toughened rubber.

▶ *This is a typical inflatable inshore rescue boat. Boats like these are bonded together by heat and glue, and are incredibly tough.*

Famous trains

- **Pullman coaches** became a byword for luxury in the USA in the 1860s.

- **After a trip to the USA,** young Belgian George Nagelmackers set up the Wagon-Lits company to do in Europe as Pullman had in the USA.

- **The most famous** Wagon-Lits was the luxurious *Orient-Express* from Paris to Istanbul, which started in 1883.

- **Among the many famous** travellers on the *Orient Express* were the female spy Mata Hari, the fictional spy James Bond and 40s film star Marlene Dietrich.

- **Another famous** Wagon-Lits train is the Trans-Siberian express, set up in 1898.

- **The Trans-Siberian** takes eight days to go right across Russia and Siberia from Moscow to Vladivostok.

> **★ STAR FACT ★**
> At 9438 km, the Trans-Siberian Express is the world's longest train journey.

▲ The Orient Express gained the glamour of intrigue as well as luxury after Agatha Christie wrote 'Murder on the Orient Express'.

- **The *Flying Scotsman*** was famed for its fast, non-stop runs from London to Edinburgh in the 1920s.

- **The *Golden Arrow*** ran from London to Paris.

- **The *Indian Pacific*** in Australia runs on the world's longest straight track, 478 km across the Nullarbor Plain.

Sailing and tacking

- **Sailing ships** can sail into the wind because the wind does not so much push the sail as suck it.

- **The sail** is always angled so that the wind blows across it, allowing it to act like the wing of an aircraft.

- **As the wind blows** over the curve of the sail, it speeds up and its pressure drops in front of the sail. The extra pressure of the other side drives the boat forward.

- **The sail** works as long as the wind is blowing straight across it, so to go in a particular direction, the sailor simply changes the angle of the sail.

- **The boat's keel,** or centreboard, stops it slipping sideways.

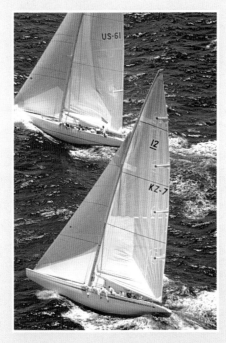

▲ With their sails in line with the hull, these yachts are sailing close to the wind.

- **The boat can sail** with the wind behind it, to the side of it or even slightly ahead of it.

- **To sail directly** or nearly directly into the wind, a boat has to 'tack'. This means zig-zagging to and fro across the path of the wind so wind is always blowing across the sails.

- **At the end** of each tack, the sail 'comes about' (changes course). The tiller (steering arm) is turned to point the boat on the new course and the sail is allowed to 'gybe' (swing over to the other side).

- **'Sailing close to the wind'** is sailing nearly into the wind.

- **'Running with the wind'** is sailing with a fast wind behind.

Airships

Rigid envelope shell

Envelope filled with helium

▼ This is a cutaway of one of the new breed of small airships made from lightweight materials and filled with safe, non-flammable helium gas.

Airbags or 'ballonets' inside the helium-filled envelope. As the airship climbs, air pressure drops and the helium expands, pushing air out of the ballonets. As the airship drops again, the helium contracts and air is let into the ballonets again

Valve to let air in and out of the ballonets

Gondola where pilot sits

Landing wheel

Propeller powered by a motor car engine

Elevator flaps to help climbing or diving

Rudder to steer the airship to the left or right

- **By the mid-1800s** ballooning was a popular activity, but balloons have to float where the wind takes them. So in 1852, French engineer Henri Giffard made a cigar-shaped balloon filled with the very light gas hydrogen. He powered it with a steam-driven propeller and added a rudder to make it more 'dirigible' or steerable.

- **In 1884** two French inventors, Charles Renard and Arthur Krebs, built the first really dirigible balloon, *La France*. This was powered by an electric motor.

- **In 1897** Austrian David Schwartz gave a powered, cigar-shaped balloon a rigid frame to create the first airship.

- **In 1900** Count Ferdinand von Zeppelin built the first of his huge airships, the 128 m long LZ-1.

- **In 1909** Zeppelin helped set up the wold's first airline, DELAG, flying 148 m long airships, carrying 10,000 passengers in their first four years.

- **In World War 1** Germany used Zeppelin airships to scout enemy positions and make the first aerial bombing raids.

- **By the 1920s** vast airships were carrying people to and fro across the Atlantic in the style of a luxury ocean-liner. The *Graf Zeppelin* flew at 130 km/h. In its gondola, 60 or more passengers sat in comfortable lounges, walked to cocktail bars or listened to bands playing.

- **On 6 May 1937** disaster struck the giant 245 m-long airship *Hindenburg* as it docked at Lakehurst, New Jersey. The hydrogen in its balloon caught fire and exploded, killing 35 people. The day of the airship was over. Hydrogen was just too dangerous.

- **In recent years** there has been a revival of airships for advertising, filled with safer helium gas. Most are non-rigid, but Airship Industries Skyship is semi-rigid and made from modern light material like carbon-fibre.

> ★ STAR FACT ★
> Fighter planes could take-off from and land on the 1930s airship *Akron* in mid-air.

Underground railways

- **Underground railways** are also called subways, metros or even just tubes.
- **There are three kinds:** open-cut; cut and cover and tube.
- **Open-cut subways** are built by digging rectangular ditches in streets, like much of New York's subway.
- **Cut-and-cover subways** are when an open-cut subway is covered again with a road or pavement.
- **Tubes** are deep, round tunnels created by boring through the ground, like most of London's lines.
- **The world's first underground** was the cut-and-cover Metropolitan Line in London, opened on 10 January 1863, using steam engines.
- **In 1890** the world's first electric tube trains ran on London's first deep tube, the City and South London.
- **After 1900** American Charles Yerkes, builder of the Chicago Loop railway, helped give London the world's most extensive tube network with 225 km of deep tubes.
- **Moscow's Metro** grand stations were built in the 1930s

▲ London was the first city in the world to have an underground system. Much of it is now in deep tube tunnels.

with marble, stained glass, statues and chandeliers.
- **New York City** has the world's largest subway network, but unlike London's most of it is quite shallow. The first line opened on 27 October 1904.

The Eiffel Tower

- **The Eiffel Tower** in Paris was 312.2 m high when it was first built. An antenna brings it up to 318.7 m. There are 1665 steps up to the top.
- **On a clear day** you can see 80 km in all directions from the top. It is often sunny at the top when the weather in the Paris streets is cloudy.
- **It was made** from 18,038 pieces of iron, held together by 2,500,000 rivets.
- **It was built in 1889** for the exhibition celebrating the 100th anniversary of the French Revolution.
- **Gustave Eiffel** (1832-1923) was the most successful engineer of the day, building not only the Eiffel Tower but New York's Statue of Liberty too.

▲ Paris's Eiffel Tower is one of the world's most famous landmarks.

- **The Eiffel Tower** was designed by Maurice Koechlin and Emile Nougier who calculated the effects of wind and gravity with amazing precision.
- **The Tower** was intended to show what could be done with cast iron.
- **During building work** Parisian artists, such as the composer Gounod and poet Maupassant, protested against its ugliness. But when completed it was an instant success with ordinary people.
- **Eiffel** was responsible for financing the construction of the tower, which cost more than $1 million.
- **When Paris was occupied** by the Nazis during the war, the lifts 'mysteriously' stopped working. They restarted the day Paris was liberated.

Missiles

★ STAR FACT ★
American Tomahawk cruise missiles could be aimed through goalposts at both ends of a football field 500 km away.

Explosive warhead

Solid rocket fuel

▶ *90% of the weight of a ballistic missile is the rocket propellant needed to reach its distant target.*

- **In AD 1232** the Chinese defended the city of K'ai-feng against the Mongols with gunpowder rockets.
- **In the early 1800s** British army officer William Congreve developed metal rockets carrying explosives.
- **In World War II** the Germans developed the first guided missiles – missiles steered to their target in flight.

- **The most frightening** German guided missiles were the V-1 flying bombs or 'doodlebugs' and the V-2 supersonic rockets. The V-2 flew at 5300 km/h.
- **Ballistic missiles** arch through the air like a thrown ball. Rockets propel them on the upward trajectory (path). They then coast down on their target. Cruise missiles are propelled by jet on a low flat path all the way.
- **In the 1950s** the USA and Soviet Union competed to develop long-range ICBMs (Intercontinental Ballistic Missiles) usually armed with nuclear warheads.
- **In the 1960s,** antiballistic missiles were developed to shoot down missiles.
- **Some ICBMs** have a range of over 5000 km. Short range missiles (SRBMs) like Pershings reach up to 500 km.
- **SAMS** (surface-to-air missiles) like Redeye are fired from the ground at aircraft. Some can be fired by a soldier with a backpack. AAMs (air-to-air missiles) like Sidewinders are fired from planes against other planes.

Ancient America

- **The largest buildings** in Ancient America were Mayan pyramids, like the Tomb of Pakal in Mexico.
- **Teotihuacan** in Mexico is one of the best preserved ancient cities in the world, with its magnificent pyramids, palaces, temples, courts and homes.
- **At its height** around 2000 years ago, Teotihuacan was the world's biggest city with 100,000 people.
- **Hopewell Indians** of Newark, Ohio built earthwork tombs in AD 250 to rival Egypt's pyramids in size.

★ STAR FACT ★
The Incas of Peru built 25,000 km of stone-paved roads between 1450 and 1532.

- **Aztecs** built the Great Temple pyramid in their ancient capital of Tenochtitlan (now Mexico City) from 1325-1500. Human sacrifices were made at the top.
- **The Mesa Verde** is a famous 'pueblos' (stone village) of the Anasazi in New Mexico, abandoned around AD 1100.
- **In the Chaco Canyon** the Anasazi built 650 km of mysterious roads to nowhere.
- **Nazca Lines** are huge outlines of birds, monkeys and other things up to 100 m across, drawn by Nazca people in the desert in S. Peru. They date from c. 100 BC to AD 700.
- **The Nazca Lines** are only clearly seen from the air. They may have been part of a giant astronomical calendar.

◀ *The 1500 year-old pyramids of the Maya were once overgrown by jungle, but most have now been restored.*

Palaces

- **The palaces** of Europe owe much to the vast palaces of the caliphs of the Near East, built in 7th and 8th centuries, with their cool courtyards and rich decoration.

- **The Topkapi Palace** in Istanbul was the sumptuous home of the Ottoman sultans for over 400 years until it was made into a museum in 1924, after the sultans' fall.

- **Venice's Doge's Palace** (mainly 1400s) shows oriental touches bought from the east by Venetian merchants.

- **The elegant Pitti Palace** in Florence was designed by the brilliant architect Brunelleschi for the merchant Luca Pitti in 1440. It was taken over by the Medici family in 1550.

- **Hampton Court Palace** southwest of London was begun in 1514 by King Henry VIII's favourite Cardinal Wolsey – but when Wolsey fell from favour, the King took it over.

- **The Escorial** in Madrid is a massive granite palace built 1563-84 by Phillip II to celebrate victories over the French.

- **Many 18th-century princes** built their own Versailles – lavish palaces like Dresden and Potsdam in Germany,

▲ *London's Buckingham Palace is the home of the Queen of Britain.*

Vienna's Schönbrunn and St Petersburg's Winter Palace.

- **Buckingham House** was built in 1702-5 for the Duke of Buckingham but remodelled as a palace in 1825.

- **Inspired by English gardens** Peter the Great made Russia's oldest garden, the Summer Garden in St Petersburg in 1710. He built the Summer Palace in it.

- **Catherine the Great** had the St Petersburg's Winter Palace built by architect Bartolomeo Rastrelli in 1762.

First steamships

- **In 1783** French nobleman Marquis Claude de Jouffroy d'Abbans built a massive steam boat that churned up the Saone River near Lyon in France for 15 minutes before the pounding engines shook it to bits.

- **In 1787** American John Fitch made the first successful steamship with an engine driving a series of paddles.

- **In 1790** Fitch started the world's first steam service on the Delaware River.

- **In 1802** Scot William Symington built a tug, the *Charlotte Dundas*, able to tow two 70-tonne barges.

- **In 1807** American Robert Fulton made the first steam passenger boats, running 240 km up the Hudson River from New York.

- **In 1819** the New York-built ship *Savannah* made the first steam-assisted crossing of the Atlantic.

- **In 1833** Canadian ship *Royal William* made the first mainly steam-powered Atlantic crossing in two days.

- **In 1843** British engineer Isembard Kingdom Brunel launched the first all-iron hull steamship, the *Great Britain*.

- **In 1858** Brunel launched *Great Eastern*, the biggest ship of the 19th century, 211 m long and weighing 30,000 tonnes.

- **Early steamships** had paddles, but in 1835 Swede John Ericsson invented a screw propeller. In 1845 a screw-driven boat won a tug-of-war with a paddle steamer.

◀ *Warships like this, HMS Theseus, were built in the 1880s.*

Taking off

- **An aircraft's wings** or 'foils' are lifted by the air flowing above and beneath them as they slice through the air.

- **Because the top** of the wing is curved, air pushed over the wing speeds up and stretches out. The stretching of the air reduces its pressure.

- **Underneath the wing** air slows down and bunches up, so air pressure here rises.

- **The wing gains 'lift'** as the wing is sucked from above and pushed from below.

★ STAR FACT ★
Slots on the wing's leading edge smooth airflow to increase the safe angle of attack.

- **The amount of lift** depends on the angle of the wing – called the angle of attack – and its shape, and also how fast it is moving through the air.

- **Aircraft** get extra lift for climbing by increasing their speed through the air and by dropping the tail so that the main wings cut through the air at a steeper angle.

- **If the angle of attack** becomes too steep, the air flow breaks up and the wing loses lift. This is called a stall.

- **Planes** take off when air is moving fast enough over the wing to provide enough lift.

- **Airliners** have 'high-lift' slots and flaps on the wings to give extra lift for slow take-off and landing speeds.

◀ The high-lift flaps are down to give extra lift on a climb.

The Taj Mahal

- **The Taj Mahal** (said *tarj m'harl*) in Agra in India is perhaps the most beautiful tomb in the world.

- **Mughal Indian** ruler Shah Jehan ordered it to be built in honour of his favourite wife Mumtaz Mahal, who died giving birth to their 14th child.

- **Mumtaz** died in 1629, and the Taj was built over 22 years from 1632 to 1653.

- **The Taj** is set at the north end of a formal Persian garden with water courses and rows of cypress trees.

- **It is made of white** marble and sits on a platform of sandstone.

- **Inside** behind an octagonal screen of alabaster marble tracery lie the jewel-inlaid

cenotaphs (tombs) of Mumtaz and Shah Jehan. The Shah was placed there when he died and his tomb is the only asymmetrical feature in the Taj.

- **20,000 workers** worked in marble and sandstone, silver, gold, carnelian, jasper, moonstone, jade, lapis lazuli and coral to enhance the Taj's beauty.

- **At each corner** of the platform is a slender minaret 40.5 m tall.

- **In the centre** is a dome 36.6 m high.

- **The main architect** was Iranian Isa Khan, but the decorations were said to be by Austin of Bordeaux and Veroneo of Venice.

◀ So perfect are the Taj's proportions that it was said to have been designed by giants and finished by jewellers.

Jet engines

Front fan to create 'cold' bypass stream

The engine casing is made of carbon-fibre and plastic honeycomb for lightness. Inside is an outer bypass duct for the 'cold-stream' of air from the front fan. An inner duct takes the 'hot stream' through the compressor, combustion chamber and turbine to create the exhaust.

Air intake

Exhaust where a hot jet of air roars out

▶ All but the very fastest warplanes are powered by turbofan jet engines, like this Russian MiG. Turbofans first came into widespread use in the 1970s and are now by far the most common kind of jet engine.

● **A kind of jet engine** was built by the Ancient Greek Hero of Alexander in the first century AD. It was a ball driven round by jets of steam escaping from two nozzles.

● **The first jet engines** were built at the same time in the 1930s by Pabst von Ohain in Germany and Frank Whittle in Britain – though neither knew of the other's work.

> ★ STAR FACT ★
> In a typical turbojet, exhaust gases roar from the engine at over 1600 km/h.

● **Ohain's engine** was put in the Heinkel HE-178 which first flew on 27 August 1939; Whittle's was put in the Gloster E28 of 1941. The first American experimental jet was the Bell XP-59 Aircomet of 1942.

● **Jets** work by pushing a jet of air out the back. This hits the air so fast that the reaction thrusts the plane forward like a deflating balloon.

● **Jet engines** are also called gas turbines because they burn fuel gas to spin the blades of a turbine non-stop.

● **Turbojets** are the original form of jet engine. Air is scooped in at the front and squeezed by spinning 'compressor' blades. Fuel sprayed into the squeezed air in the middle of the engine burns, making the mixture expand dramatically. The expanding air not only pushes round turbines which drive the compressor, but also sends out a high-speed jet of hot air to propel the plane. This high-speed jet is noisy but good for ultra-fast warplanes and supersonic aircraft.

● **Turboprops** are turbojets that use most of their power to turn a propeller rather than force out a hot air jet.

● **Turbofans** are used by most airliners because they are

quieter and cheaper to run. In these, extra turbines turn a huge fan at the front. Air driven by this fan bypasses the engine core and gives a huge extra boost at low speeds.

● **Ramjets** or 'flying stovepipes' are the simplest type of jet engine, used only on missiles. They dispense with both compressor and turbine blades and simply rely on the speed of the jet through the air to ram air in through the intake into the engine.

▶ Like nearly all warplanes today, 'stealth' aircraft are jet-propelled. But the afterburner stream of hot gases from the jets provides a 'signature' that can show up all too clearly on some detection equipment. So stealth aircraft are designed to 'supercruise' – that is, fly at supersonic speeds without much afterburn.

Yachts and catamarans

▲ *Catamarans with twin hulls and outriggers (extra floats) are all developed from traditional Polynesian outriggers.*

- **The word yacht** comes from the 17th-century Dutch word *jacht*, which meant 'ship for chasing'.

- **English yachting** began in 1662 when King Charles II raced his brother James from Greenwich for a £100 bet in a small pleasure boat given to him by the Dutch.

- **In 1898** Joshua Slocum sailed single-handed round the world in the 11.3 m *Spray*, proving the seaworthiness of small craft.

- **From the 1920s** the same aerodynamic principles applied to hulls were used for sails and rigging.

- **Most racing yachts** are now built from aluminium and light, strong composites such as carbon-fibre.

- **In the 1960s** twin-hulled catamarans became popular since they pierce waves well yet are wide and stable.

- **In 1983** Australian Ben Lexcen became the first non-American to win the famous America's Cup race.

- **The key to Lexcen's** success was revolutionary winglets on the keel to improve stability.

- **Sails on some yachts** are now computer controlled to keep them at exactly the right angle.

> **! NEWS FLASH !**
> America's Cup yachts have winglets on their rudder and keels for extra stability.

Powerboats

- **Powerboating** began in 1863 when Frenchman Jean Lenoir installed a petrol engine in a small boat.

- **The first major race** was in 1903 across the English Channel. The Gold Cup of the American Power Boat Association (APBA) started on the Hudson in 1904.

- **About 1910** motor makers like Evinrude introduced detachable 'outboard' motors that clamp to the stern. Inboard motors have the engine built into the hull.

- **In the 1920s** racing boats adopted 'planing hulls' for skimming across the water at high speeds, rather than traditional deep v-shaped 'displacement' hulls.

▼ *Powerboat racing has become hugely competitive like motor racing, and Formula 1 boats roar round at speeds over 200 km/h.*

After World War II hulls were made more and more, not from wood, but metals and fibreglass.

- **Most powerboats** are driven, not by a propeller screw, but a high-speed jet of water.

- **In 1994** American Tom Gentry set the offshore Class 1 record of 253.35 km/h in Skater powerboats.

- **In 1996** Gentry's *Gentry Eagle* crossed the Atlantic in 2 days 14 hours 7 mins. In 1997, the *Destriero* made it in 2 days 6 hours 34 minutes.

- **The official water speed** record is 511.11 km/h by Kenneth Warby in his hydroplane *Spirit of Australia* on Blowering Lake, New South Wales on 8 October 1978.

- **Jet skis** are like motorboats that skim across the water on a ski. They were developed by the American Clayton Jacobsen back in the 1960s.

- **The jet ski** speed record is 69 km/h by French D. Condemine in 1994 on a Yahama.

Biplanes

- **Most early planes** were biplanes (double-wingers) or even triplanes (triple-wingers).

- **Monoplanes** (single-wingers) like Blériot's (see record breaking flights) were fast and won many early races – because they did not drag on the air like multi-wings.

- **Accidents** by overstressed competition monoplanes made it look as if they were dangerous. Single wings were weak, it seemed, because they had to be very long to give a similar lifting area to multi-wings.

- **In 1912** the French and British banned monoplanes, so all World War I fighter planes were multi-wingers.

- **Biplane wings** were strong because struts and wires linked the small, light wings to combine their strength.

- **Famous World War I** fighters included the British Sopwith Camel and Bristol Fighter.

◀ The biplanes of World War I were slow but highly manoeuvrable. Pilots were able to show tremendous flying skill in the first aerial 'dog fights' between planes.

- **The Fokker triplane** flown by German air ace Baron von Richtofen (the Red Baron) was said to be 'fearsome to look at and climbs like a lift'.

- **With their network** of struts and wires, biplanes were affectionately known as 'string bags'.

- **In the years** after World War I, huge biplane airliners were built including the Handley Page Heracles of the 1930s.

- **By the late 1920s** planes could be built strongly all in metal. So to cut drag and boost speed, designers went back to monoplanes with planes like the Supermarine S6B. Soon biplanes seemed old-fashioned.

The Palace of Versailles

▲ Versailles is perhaps the most expensive palace ever built.

- **Versailles,** in France, is a magnificent palace built for Louis XIV. Work began in 1661 and carried on for a century.

- **When complete** Versailles was 500 m long, had over 1300 major rooms and could accommodate 5000 people.

- **The first architect** was Louis le Vau but Jules Hardouin-Mansart took over in 1676, adding the second storey.

- **The interior** was conceived by Charles le Brun. His Hall of Mirrors is a long hall lined with mirrors. A masterly painted ceiling shows Louis XIV's achievements.

- **Throughout Versailles** high ceilings and great doors are emblazoned in gold with the mark of the sun god, Apollo – and of King Louis, known as the Sun King.

- **The huge gardens** of tree-lined terraces and ponds were landscaped by Andre le Notre with 1400 fountains, 400 new pieces of sculpture and four million tulips.

- **The fountains** appear 'magically' still to show the power of the king over nature.

- **The palace** had a famous state-of-the-art theatre designed by Jacques-Ange Gabriel in 1769.

- **During the French Revolution** on 6 October 1789, mobs invaded the palace and wrecked its interiors. Restoration began in 1837 and has continued ever since.

- **The avenues of Washington DC** were laid out in imitation of Versailles by a French architect.

Trains of the future

▲ Many cities now have short monorails, but they seem unlikely to get much bigger because of the disruption building would cause.

- **Monorails** are single beam tracks raised over city streets.

- **The first monorail** was built in Wuppertal in Germany as long ago as 1901 and monorails have been seen as trains of the future ever since.

- **Monorails** of the future may be air-cushion trains or maglev, as at Birmingham airport.

- **A maglev** is proposed in Japan to take passengers the 515 km from Tokyo to Osaka in under 60 minutes. Germany is planning a system called Transrapid.

- **PRT** or Personalized Rapid Transport is automatic cars on monorails. AGT (Automated Guideway Transit) is the same for coaches, as in Detroit, or London's DLR.

- **300 km/h plus** High Speed Train (HST) systems like the French TGV are being built in many places, such as from Moscow to St Petersburg.

- **In 2004** the 320 km/h Tampa-Miami Florida Overland Express opens. The same year a 4500 km 300 km/h line may open from Melbourne to Darwin, Australia.

- **Most HSTs** run on special straight tracks. Tilting trains lean into bends to give high speeds on winding old tracks.

- **Tilting trains** include the 300 km/h Italian Fiat Pendolini and the Swedish X2000.

- **From 2000** the 240 km/h tilting train *The American Flyer* – Washington to Baltimore – is the USA's fastest train.

Rockets

> **· STAR FACT ·**
> The *Saturn V* rocket that launched the Apollo mission to the Moon is the most powerful rocket ever built.

- **Rockets** work by burning fuel. As fuel burns and swells out behind, the swelling pushes the rocket forward.

- **Solid-fuel rockets** are the oldest of all engines, used by the Chinese a thousand years ago.

- **Solid-fuel engines** are basically rods of solid, rubbery

◀ Only powerful rockets can give the thrust to overcome gravity and launch spacecraft into space. They fall away in stages once the spacecraft is travelling fast enough.

fuel with a tube down the middle. When the fuel is set alight it burns out through the fuel until all is used.

- **Solid fuel** rockets are usually only used for model rockets and small booster rockets. But the Space Shuttle has two solid rocket boosters (SRBs) as well as three main liquid fuel engines.

- **Most powerful launch rockets** use liquid fuel. The Shuttle uses hydrogen. Other fuels include kerosene.

- **Liquid fuel** only burns with oxygen, so rockets must also carry an oxidizer (a substance that gives oxygen) such as liquid oxygen (LOX) or nitrogen tetroxide.

- **Future rocket drives** include nuclear thermal engines that use a nuclear reactor to heat the gas blasted out.

- **NASA's Deep Space-1** project is based on xenon ion engines which thrust, not hot gases out the back, but electrically charged particles called ions.

- **Solar thermal engines** of the future would collect the Sun's rays with a large mirror to heat gases.

Navigation

- **Early sailors** found their way by staying near land, looking for 'landmarks' on shore. Away from land they steered by stars, so had only a vague idea of direction in the day.

- **After 1100** European sailors used a magnetic compass needle to find North.

- **A compass** only gives you a direction to steer; it does not tell you where you are.

- **The astrolabe** was used from c.1350. This measured the angle of stars above the horizon, or the Sun at noon giving an idea of latitude (how far north or south of the equator).

- **From the 1500s** the cross-staff gave a more accurate measure of latitude at night from the angle between the Pole Star and the horizon.

- **From the mid-1700s** until the 1950s, sailors measured latitude with a mirror sextant. This had two mirrors. It gave the angle of a star (or the Sun) when

◄ *A navigational instrument for measuring latitude from the angle of certain stars.*

one mirror was adjusted until the star was at horizon height in the other.

- **For centuries** the way to find longitude – how far east or west – was by dead reckoning. This meant trailing a knotted rope in the water to calculate speed, and so estimate how far you had come.

- **You can find longitude** by comparing the Sun's height with its height at the same time at a longitude you know. But early pendulum clocks did not work well enough aboard ship to give the correct time.

- **The longitude problem** was solved when John Harrison made a very accurate spring-driven clock or chronometer.

- **Ships** can now find their position with pinpoint accuracy using the Global Positioning System or GPS. This works by electronically comparing signals from a ring of satellites.

Sydney Opera House

▲ *Standing by the water's edge in Sydney Harbour, Sydney Opera House is one of the world's most distinctive buildings.*

- **Sydney Opera House** in Sydney, opened in October 1973, is one of Australia's best known landmarks.

- **The design** by Danish architect Jorn Utzon was agreed in January after a competition involving 233 entries, but it took 14 years to build.

- **The radical sail-like** roofs were said to have been inspired by sea shells.

- **The original design** was so unusual that it proved impossible to build structurally, so Utzon altered the shape of the roofs to base them on sections of a ball.

- **The altered design** meant the roofs could be made from pre-cast concrete slabs.

- **The roofs** were made from 2194 pre-cast concrete slabs, weighing up to 15 tonnes each.

- **The slabs** are tied together with 350 km of tensioned steel cable and covered with 1 million Swedish tiles.

- **In the mouths of the roofs** are 6225 sq m of French glass in double layers, one tinted topaz-colour.

- **Inside** there were originally four theatres – the Concert Hall, the Opera Theatre, the Drama Theatre and the Playhouse.

- **A new theatre, The Studio,** was added in March 1999 for small cast plays and films.

Bombers of World War II

- **In the 1930s** Boeing built the B-17 'Flying Fortress', with gun turrets to battle its way through to targets even by day.

- **The 1929** Curtis F8C Helldiver was the first 'dive-bomber' – designed to drop its bombs at the end of a long dive on targets like aircraft carriers. German 'Stuka' dive-bombers gained a fearsome name in the German invasions of 1939.

- **The twin-engined** Heinkel 111, Dornier D017 and Junkers Ju88 were the main German bombers in the *Blitzkrieg* (literally 'lightning war') raids of the Battle of Britain.

- **In December 1939** the heavy loss of British Wellingtons showed that lightly armed bombers could not sustain daylight raids, so the British switched to night raids.

- **Blind bombing** radar systems like the Hs2, and flare trails left by advance 'Pathfinder' missions, improved accuracy on night raids.

◀ *The British Avro Lancaster could carry 6000 kg of bombs on low altitude raids.*

- **The ultra-light** De Havilland Mosquito was fast enough to fly daylight raids.

- **The Russian Ilyushin Il-2** or Stormovik was so good at bombing tanks Stalin said it was 'as necessary to the Red Army as air or bread.'

- **The dambusters** were the Lancasters of 617 squadron of 1943 that attacked German dams with 'bouncing bombs'. These were round bombs designed by Barnes Wallis that bounced over the water surface towards the target dams.

- **Kamikaze** (Japanese for 'divine wind') were fighters loaded with bombs and gasoline which their pilots aimed in suicide dives at enemy ships.

- **The biggest bomber** was the Boeing B-29 Superfortress which could fly over 10,000 m up. In 1945, B-29s dropped the atomic bombs on Hiroshima and Nagasaki in Japan.

Early cars

- **In 1890** Frenchman Emile Levassor made the first real car, with an engine at the front. He laughed, saying, *C'est brutal, mais ca marche* ('It's rough, but it goes'.)

- **The Duryea** brothers made the first successful American car in 1893.

- **Early accidents** made cars seem dangerous. Until 1896 in Britain and 1901 in New York cars had to be preceded by a man on foot waving a red flag.

- **In 1895** the French Panhard-Levassor company made the first covered 'saloon' car.

- **In 1898** Renault drove the wheels with a shaft not a chain.

- **The Oldsmobile** Curved Dash of 1900 was the first car to sell in thousands.

- **On early cars** speed was controlled by moving a small ignition advance lever backwards or forwards.

- **Dirt roads,** oil spray and noise meant early motorists needed protective clothing such as goggles and earmuffs.

- **The first cars** had wooden or wire spoked wheels. Pressed steel wheels like today's came in after 1945.

- **In 1906** an American steam-driven car, the Stanley Steamer, broke the land speed record at over 205 kmh.

◀ *By 1904, many cars were starting to have the familiar layout of cars today – engine at the front, driver on one side, steering wheel, petrol tank at the back, a shaft to drive the wheels and so on.*

Canals

- **In 1470 BC** the Egyptian Pharaoh Sesostris had the first Suez Canal built, linking the Mediterranean and Red Sea.

- **The Grand Canal** in China is the world's longest man-made waterway, running 1747 km west of Beijing.

- **The origins** of the Grand Canal date to the 4th century BC, but it was rebuilt in AD 607.

- **The late 1700s and early 1800s** saw many canals built for the factories of the Industrial Revolution, like James Brindley's Bridgwater Canal in Lancashire, England.

- **Clinton's Folly** is the Erie Canal linking Lake Erie to the Hudson in the USA, pushed through by governor De Witt Clinton in 1825.

- **The current Suez Canal** was built by Ferdinand de Lesseps (1859-1869). It is the world's longest big-ship canal, 161.9 km long.

- **The Panama Canal** links the Atlantic and Pacific Oceans 82 km across Central America, and cutting the sea journey from New York to San Francisco by 14,400 km.

▲ Amsterdam's canals were dug in the city's heyday in the 1600s.

- **The Panama Canal** takes over 400 million tonnes of shipping a year – more than any other canal.

- **The world's busiest canal** is Germany's Kiel which takes 45,000 ships a year from the North Sea to the Baltic.

- **In Russia** one of the world's longest canal systems links the Black Sea to the Arctic Ocean via the Volga River.

Airliners

- **The Boeing 247** of 1933 was the world's first modern airliner, with smooth monoplane wings, streamlined metal body and retractable landing wheels.

- **The Douglas DC-3** of 1936 could carry 21 passengers smoothly at 320 km/h and was the first popular airliner.

- **In 1952** the world's first jet airliner, the De Havilland Comet 1 came into service.

- **The Comet** more than halved international flight times but several tragic accidents led to its grounding in 1954.

▶ The four-engined Boeing 747 flies at 10–13,000 m – well above most storms – and can fly non-stop from New York to Tokyo.

! NEWS FLASH !
Spaceplanes like Lockheed-Martin's *Venture Star* may make space trips routine flights.

- **The age of jet** air travel really began with the American Boeing 707 and Douglas DC-8 of the late 1950s.

- **The Boeing 747** jumbo jet of 1970 – the first 'wide-bodied jet' – had over 400 seats, making air travel cheap.

- **Four-engined jets** like the 747 can fly 10,000 km non-stop at speeds of 1000 km/h. Two and three-engine jets like the DC-10 make shorter flights.

- **Supersonic airliners** able to travel at over 2000 km/h like the Russian Tupolev Tu-144 have proved too heavy on fuel and too noisy.

- **The planned 555-seat Airbus** A380 would be the first full-length double-deck airliner.

INDEX

Acknowledgements

Artists: Terry Riley, Peter Sarson

The publishers would like to thank the following sources for the photographs used in this book:

Page 9 (T/R) CORBIS; Page 11 (T/L) Steve Lindridge, Eye Ubiquitous/CORBIS; Page 14 (B/L) Richard T. Nowitz/CORBIS; Page 25 (B/L) CORBIS; Page 38 (B/L) Jim Sugar Photography/CORBIS; Page 41 (B/R) Joseph Sohm, ChromoSohm Inc./CORBIS; Page 43 (T/R) In-press photography; Page 49 (T/R) Wolfgang Kaehler/CORBIS

All other photographs are from MKP Archives